T0209713

Connecting Within

A MOTHER'S JOURNEY
TO BALANCE, PEACE AND JOY

Jennie Askins

BALBOA.
PRESS

A DIVISION OF HAY HOUSE

Copyright © 2019 Jennie Askins.

All rights reserved. No part of this book may be used or reproduced by any means, graphic, electronic, or mechanical, including photocopying, recording, taping or by any information storage retrieval system without the written permission of the author except in the case of brief quotations embodied in critical articles and reviews.

Balboa Press books may be ordered through booksellers or by contacting:

Balboa Press
A Division of Hay House
1663 Liberty Drive
Bloomington, IN 47403
www.balboapress.com
1 (877) 407-4847

Because of the dynamic nature of the Internet, any web addresses or links contained in this book may have changed since publication and may no longer be valid. The views expressed in this work are solely those of the author and do not necessarily reflect the views of the publisher, and the publisher hereby disclaims any responsibility for them.

The author of this book does not dispense medical advice or prescribe the use of any technique as a form of treatment for physical, emotional, or medical problems without the advice of a physician, either directly or indirectly. The intent of the author is only to offer information of a general nature to help you in your quest for emotional and spiritual well-being. In the event you use any of the information in this book for yourself, which is your constitutional right, the author and the publisher assume no responsibility for your actions.

Any people depicted in stock imagery provided by Getty Images are models, and such images are being used for illustrative purposes only.
Certain stock imagery © Getty Images.

Print information available on the last page.

Interior Image Credit: Jennie Irving

ISBN: 978-1-9822-3210-8 (sc)
ISBN: 978-1-9822-3211-5 (e)

Balboa Press rev. date: 08/23/2019

I dedicate this book to my two beautiful daughters Viviana and Abriana and to my parents who have always been my rock.

Contents

Introduction

"Loving oneself is the beginning of a lifelong romance."—Oscar Wilde

I came from a very loving home. I was raised by, and grew up with, a mother and a father. My dad worked all the time; he was barely home except on Sundays. My dad worked very hard and was the main financial provider.

The burden of running the household rested on my mother's shoulders. My mom wanted to conquer the world and do everything on her own. My mother is very Type A personality, very perfectionistic. She did not know how to ask for help and did not want to. Growing up, that brought on a lot of stress for me. I had a hard time relaxing.

So there I was at age 32 bringing my beautiful baby home from the hospital. The day I gave birth to my daughter was the happiest day of my life. She was a precious gem to me. I was afraid if I made the wrong move, she would break, or I would do something that could damage her forever. I had this fear of failing, of royally messing up. I was so scared and riddled with anxiety but at the same time had so much joy, meaning, and happiness as I have never felt before. It's normal for a new mom to feel these mixed emotions but when emotions are controlled by fear, something is wrong. It's time to look within. That's what I did; I realized I was creating my own anxiety.

The only role model I had was how my mother raised me. Yes, I was raised with love, but my mom deserved sainthood for the effort she made on behalf of her family. It seemed she carried the burdens of ten people and never asked for help. When I brought my daughter home, I wondered would I have to give up everything as my mom did and be the martyr for my family? Would it not be OK to ask for help, and if I did ask for help would that be a sign I was failing as a mom? These questions were swimming around in my head. Fear and negativity filled my thoughts.

I found myself completely exhausted, stressed, and unhappy. I thought:

Is this what being a mother is, giving up all self-care? That's all I knew at the time because that's the example I had.

Within the first year of bringing my daughter home I began to be depressed. I was anxious all the time and my head wasn't clear enough to figure out why, especially on the little sleep I was getting. My marriage was also suffering. The sad truth came one day when we both realized we couldn't do it together any longer. We are divorced now, but we are both a lot happier.

During this struggle, I started searching my soul; I would wake and stay up all hours of the night. I kept asking myself the burning question: Why am I so depressed; why am I so anxious? Finally, after months of this reoccurring thought, it clicked:

I have completely let myself go! I don't know who I am any longer. I know I am a different person now because I am a mother and my life has completely changed, but I don't even feel like a person anymore. I feel like a walking zombie. I feel like I don't matter.

It was such a scary thought process, but also the great awakening I needed. Yes, this baby needs me and I love her more than life itself, but how am I going to be any good to her and take care of her if I am not at all taking care of myself? Do I want her to bring home *her* new baby one day and struggle to the point of absolute exhaustion because that's what she saw me do throughout her childhood?

The answer to these two questions is of course: No! I want her to be happy, confident, strong, and content and not feel she has to be perfect or conquer the world. I want my daughter to be the best she can be and know she's only one person with limited resources and it's OK to need help… it's OK to rest and take care of yourself, even when you bring home a new baby. I think mothers who never learn the skill of taking care of themselves during those child-raising years feel a sense of resentment, robbed in some way. I'm here to tell you, you don't have to feel like that; you shouldn't feel like that. What makes you a good and loving mother is a mother who makes sure she is taking time out for herself. When you try to conquer the world, the only thing that will happen is exhaustion, depression, resentment, and anxiety.

How we grew up has a lot to do with how we are going to raise our own children. Some of us do the opposite of our parents and some of us follow suit. It really slaps you in the face the day you take home your precious baby from the hospital, because most of us have a lot of unhealed issues from our own upbringing. You start going over your own childhood. I started to understand my childhood more fully and the struggles my mother carried, once I had my own family. Having kids of my own did give me a new appreciation for my mom. She was a great mother and loved me and my two brothers more than anything and still does.

I can tell you it's important to put your children first and foremost, make them your Number One priority because our babies don't ask to be born and they need us. The younger they are, the more they need you, but I can tell you to make sure you are taking care of yourself and making time for self-care. If you don't, it will affect your child(ren) in a negative way.

The earlier you start this as a mother, the better off you will be. Happy mom, happy kids! The more you take time to give to you, the more resources you will have to give to them. It won't come from a place of exhaustion and deprivation.

There is a reason why, when you are on a plane, they say to put your oxygen mask on first. If you put a mask on your children first and something happens to you, you may not be there to save them or care for them. It's the same in our everyday life. If you are the martyr giving to the point of exhaustion and not making time for self-care or loving yourself enough, then you will have little left to give to them.

Don't you want to be giving to them happily? Otherwise, I believe you will start feeling like a robot who is just going through the motions and that's not how motherhood should be. I know we will all have days we feel like we are going through the motions and we have reached our max, but when that becomes your mere existence, it's time for some changes. If you aren't being a good example for your children, you are teaching them to not care for themselves, and you will also act out in anger, sadness, loneliness, and resentment. Not taking care of yourself as a parent over the long run won't lead to being a good example to them.

Mothers who care for themselves and take time out every day for some self-care, have a beautiful glow to them. The younger your children are, the harder it is to care for yourself, but you must give it your best effort. Remember parenthood isn't a one-person job and I do believe: It takes a village to raise a child.

Some women think it's selfish to take care of themselves; but there is a bad way to be selfish, and also a healthy way. Deep down we know the difference. You have to make taking care of you a priority and habit. The earlier you start doing that, the better off you will be and the better off your children will be. If you love your kids, then you will take care of yourself.

On the days I don't take any time for me, I am antsy, I yell at my kids, and I am more irritable and snappy. I can feel my body and face are tense. I feel worn out, like I am going through the motions but not really enjoying them. Then on those nights, when I go to bed, I feel guilty, because they either got yelled at all day or I didn't really mother from my heart but rather from a place of deprivation and pure exhaustion.

Now that I do take time for myself, I notice the difference. Don't get me wrong—I still struggle with this like anyone else. I still have moments I don't want to ask for help or I neglect myself. But I am aware of it now and I don't let it go on for too long. I don't want to go back to that dark place of anxiety and depression. Let's stop living as if everyone else but us is important. As kids get older, they will have less respect for their parents and maybe even take advantage of them, especially mothers whom they see not taking care of themselves. Or they feel pity for you and who wants that?

As a mother raising two daughters, I want them to look up to me. I want them to see a strong capable woman with dreams and goals. I choose to be the good example for them on self-love and care. I want my girls to remember happiness on my face and big smiles when we look at each other. I want to be that example for them.

Drop the perfectionism. Drop the idea of having to do everything by yourself. Drop the idea that you don't matter as much as your children. You do matter. You are deserving, just as much as anybody else. Let people help. Let people care for you, but most of all, be the one who cares for you. You matter, and trust me, your kids think so, too. You are the most important person in their world. They want their mom to be good emotionally, mentally, and physically. That's the greatest gift you can give to them.

Running yourself down and being under stress can also bring on illness. If you get sick, or something happens to you, who is going to take care of your precious babies? Taking care of yourself is part of taking care of your kids!

Start today. You're worth it!

Chapter 1

—❧

STEP 1: LOOKING AND FEELING FABULOUS

"There is only one corner of the universe you can be certain of improving, and that's your own self."—Aldous Huxley

As a mother, I know it is sometimes hard for us to take care of ourselves, and the smaller your children are, the harder it is. Sometimes even taking a shower is an effort. My kids are very small and some days I don't even get to take a shower until later in the day or not at all. On the days I don't shower or fix myself up a little, I feel *blah*. I don't want to leave the house, I yell at my girls, and I eat more junk food. I can't wait for the day to be over, and I have less than a smile on my face.

Showering, putting a good moisturizer on your face, and combing your hair make you feel more like a woman, a human being. I notice on days I am not put together, people respond to me differently. Subconsciously, we are aware of that and that alone can throw your day off. Whether we want to admit it or not, we do care what others think.

When we have little ones running around, it is very easy to feel stressed and worn down. Some days I look at my face and I think: *Wow, do I look worn out*! One of the best things we can do for ourselves every day, is to look into the mirror and tell ourselves how beautiful we are and point out the great features we see on our faces. We should do this exercise with our bodies, too.

Right now you may not be able to think of anything good about your appearance, but I say: Yes, you can! It was hard for me to do this at first, but the more I do it, the more I appreciate myself. So it's important to appreciate who you are as a woman.

Yes, it's hard to feel like a soft, sexy, attractive woman, when you are constantly cleaning up after your little ones, running around like you're a taxi driver, packing lunches, putting dinner on the table, etc.

Finding a minute to brush your teeth or brush your hair can be challenging when you're raising kids. To feel good on the inside, I believe we all must take care of the outside, too. You aren't just a mother—you are a human being... a woman. Even on the days that are hectic when you have little time, make it a point to shower, put a good moisturizer on your face, and add a beautiful-smelling body lotion or perfume. Research shows that the way we feel about ourselves plays a huge role in the way we react to others... including our children.

Feeling like a woman, and not only a mother, is very important to your mental state. You matter. Your kids think so, and you need to think so, too. You may wonder, *How am I supposed to feel like a woman when I constantly change diapers, have kids hanging on me, breast feed, have a whole house to clean, and have meals to prepare?* As mothers to young ones we get spit up on, peed on... and the list goes on. We dry crying eyes, wipe snot from noses, and more. You may work full or part time. You think: *I'm supposed to feel beautiful, sexy....* Not even close.

It can be done. I know some days it can be tough, because I constantly struggle with this myself and at times feel I have no energy left for me; but that's where the big **I MATTER. I am still a WOMAN** has to come into play. Positive self-talk is key. Over time, constant positive self-talk will change your brain waves.

Let's start with our daily shower. Showering daily is most important to feeling good. Sometimes stay-at-home moms can be the worst with this because we don't have anywhere special we have to be. It's easy for us stay-at-home moms to think: *I am so tired today—skipping a shower and staying in my pajamas sounds like a great plan.*

It's OK to have a day like this once in a while. Sometimes we *need* a day like this.

But living day after day and not caring what you look like while raising your children is more detrimental for us than good. Feeling beautiful doesn't just happen... we women must make it happen. Remember we set the example for our kids. If you have a daughter, you are teaching her by example how to take care of herself when she becomes a mother someday, or you're teaching her how NOT to take care of herself.

Start your day with a nice hot shower, or, if you need extra time in the morning take your shower the night before you go to bed so you aren't rushing in the morning. Next, smile at yourself in the mirror and say out loud, "I MATTER AND I AM BEAUTIFUL." Follow this with another positive statement that starts with "I AM…" When you give yourself positive self-talk, it motivates you to want to take better care of yourself.

Then look at your clothes. Yoga pants and T-shirts or sweatshirts are the go-to attire for stay-at-home moms. I got stuck in that trend because it's an outfit that is easy, cozy, and looks good. But then I realized I was eating more than I should because my elastic yoga pants are loose around my belly when I am already full and still stuffing my face. So I decided: no more daily yoga pants for me, except when I go to the gym.

Instead, I put on a cute, stylish pair of jeans with a nice shirt and I am ready to roll. I also love to wear dresses; they make me feel more feminine. I always feel good in a dress, so I buy casual dresses to wear. Only you know what makes you feel good, so wear something you are comfortable in and feel good in. Wear something other than pajamas or gym clothes. I guarantee you will notice a difference in how you feel.

As for your face, I mentioned earlier a good moisturizer goes a long way and so does a great cleanser. Think about giving yourself a face mask once or twice a week. Most masks stay on for 10-20 minutes, and once you take them off, your skin will feel renewed and refreshed.

Some of us wear makeup; some of us don't. If you don't wear makeup, simply take care of your skin and you will have a healthy natural radiant glow. Some light gloss goes a long way. I personally love makeup since it makes me feel more feminine.

Sometimes we don't have a lot of time to put on our full face. At times like this, a good lipstick, mascara, eyebrow pencil, and some color on your cheeks can go a long way in only five minutes. Your eyebrows frame your face, mascara adds definition to your eyes, blush gives your cheeks a healthy glow, and lip gloss or lipstick completes the look. So now we are showered, dressed neat, have some makeup on or are fresh faced, and we are ready to start our day! As for our hair, as long as it's clean and neat, it can be loose or collected in a braid or ponytail.

When we feel good about our outer appearance, we can often accomplish more in our day. When we feel good about ourselves, we treat our kids better. For us stay-at-home moms, we are ready to go out and do more things with our kids. We don't just stay home and let them watch TV all day and make messes all over our house. We aren't as short-fused with them, because we feel good. As women, we have many facets. When we feel good, we start tapping in to them.

I am a single mother now. I was married for almost seven years. When my second daughter was not even a month old, my husband and I decided to call it quits.

My marriage didn't work out for multiple reasons, but the one thing I always knew was that when a woman starts having children, the thing the husband fears the most is weight gain and his wife not dressing up for him any longer. Becoming only a mother and not a wife is very detrimental to a marriage, especially if a wife/mother lets herself go.

Before I got pregnant with my second daughter, I would make sure to look good every day. I am not saying when you have a baby you need to immediately lose weight and put your full face on daily. But as you adjust to motherhood and time passes, your husband is going to want to see the woman he fell in love with. Men are visual. It's not appealing to them and doesn't make them want to run home to a woman who doesn't brush her hair, brush her teeth, shower, or change from sweat pants all day.

A man wants to feel like he is with his woman, and not just the mother of his children. He wants to feel desired, and he wants to desire his wife. He wants to come home to a wife who is happy and takes great care of herself. The more you take care of yourself, the more he will love and respect you. Trust me on that.

It is important to still go on dates with your husband. If you are a single mom like me, it is still important to go on dates. Even if you aren't ready for a serious commitment, date! Have fun! Once a month set aside time for just the two of you where you dress up, go out on a date, and make some new loving memories with one another. Keep those flames burning bright by trying new things together, spending alone time whenever and wherever you can, sharing dreams, and making new dreams together. Going on dates and looking good makes you feel like a desired woman and makes him feel good as a man.

Having a loving healthy relationship with your husband or significant other is important to your kids. It shows them a good example of what two people who love each other act like.

For you single moms, even if you aren't looking to get into a serious relationship right now, it's important that you still stay in the dating world. It's important to dress up and try to go on at least one date a month. If for some reason that's not practical or feasible, or you have no interest in dating, plan a night out at least once a month with a friend. As a single mother, it's important to stay connected to the outside world and have a life other than work and raising kids. Nobody makes us feel more like a woman than a man so surround yourself with some men, even if they are only friends. It will help you stay in touch with your feminine side.

As single moms, we tend to do more for our kids and have less time for ourselves because we are only one person. If we try to look our best each day, we will feel better and we will receive better. The Universe gives us what we are feeling. If we're feeling bad or blah, we get blah. When we feel good and look our best, good things happen.

My dad used to say, "Activity makes activity." When you're going out and need time to yourself to get ready and look good, don't hesitate to have a babysitter arrive earlier than the time you need to leave, or ask to drop your kids off a little earlier than normal at their dad's so you can take your time and get ready without having to rush. That will put you in a better frame of mind and help make for a more relaxing night! Don't feel guilty doing this. You deserve time for yourself. You deserve a night out.

We talk about day-to-day stuff and how to feel better about ourselves on the outside, but I can't overlook one of the most important things and that's diet and exercise. When I say diet, I am not referring to diet as in losing weight; I am referring to eating right. Give yourself the proper nutrients you need to function on a daily basis. What we eat has a huge effect on our appearance, our moods, and of course our waistline. It's important to take a daily vitamin, especially if we skip meals, lack sleep, or are overworked and overstressed. Daily vitamins will help us keep things in balance.

I keep a food diary every day, right on my phone. I mark down what I eat so I don't overeat and I can maintain my weight, but I also do it because it helps me make sure I am eating healthy food. Our kids look to us for proper eating habits. The better you eat, the better you feel. Find what works for you but it's good to try and eat healthy. Your hair will shine, your skin will glow, your figure will stay in form, and your kids will be learning healthy eating.

It is extremely important that you have some kind of exercise regime even if it's walking 10 minutes a day or jogging in place five minutes a day. Even a little bit of exercise is better than none.

You don't have to do it alone. If you don't have time to belong to a gym or get away for a little exercise, then do it with your children. Make exercise a fun family activity. If your kids are old enough, go out for a family run or power walk while they ride bikes or rollerblade. Or go to an indoor place to climb a rock wall. There are many ways to exercise as a family if you can't find time to do it alone, or don't want to do it alone.

Another fun thing my girls and I do sometimes is dance in the living room, and I work up a serious sweat. It's good for kids to see exercise at a young age; that way, exercise becomes a normal part of life. The younger our kids are aware of this, the better. The more active kids are, the more they learn to love their bodies. The more active we are, the more we learn to love our bodies, appreciate our bodies, and feel the body-mind connection.

Walking around the house in pajamas all day or not brushing your hair or teeth isn't going to make you a better or more productive mom. All the things we do matter. Our kids are watching; they're taking it all in. When they see how you feel about your appearance, the better they will feel about their appearance. I am talking about little girls here. Research shows that how a girl feels about her appearance is largely determined by how her mother regards her own appearance.

In a recent United Kingdom Dove survey of 2,000 moms, girls as young as seven years old were reported to mimic their moms' behaviors… like sucking in their stomachs or describing themselves as fat. They are always listening to what you say about yourself.

As for little boys, they observe, too, but in a different way. Some say boys choose women like their mothers. You are not only teaching your daughter how to love and take care of herself, you're teaching your sons this as well.

CHALLENGE: If you're someone who doesn't usually fix yourself up, try it for a week straight, every day. At the end of each day, journal how you feel about yourself and about your day. I bet you will notice a big difference that week in your mood, in the way you treat your kids and your spouse/significant other, and in the way you treat yourself.

BREATHING AWARENESS MEDITATION:

Close your eyes.
Bring awareness to the breath.
Breathe in for three.
Breathe out for five.
Follow the inhale and exhale.
Mentally repeat to yourself these words:
I am beautiful inside and out.
I accept myself for who I am.
I am love and light.
Everything that happens to me is for my greater good.
Repeat these phrases three times each.
Slowly open your eyes…
SMILE—feel the smile go through your entire being.

Chapter 2

STEP 2: PEACE BEGINS WITH ME

*"Every day may not be good, but there is something
good in every day."—Unknown*

For the last two months, I haven't touched writing until now. I can honestly tell you these last few months have been stressful for one reason or another and the spiritual side of me can't help but think I was being tested. Yeah, you want to write about inner peace… well, here is some stress for you, so de-stress! Anyway, that's how I have felt these last couple of months; but sure enough, here I am ready to write this chapter on finding inner peace.

We are all human, so even the calmest and most peaceful people can feel anxious at times. It has taken me a long time to find a good way of de-stressing. Still, I get anxious and feel twisted inside with all kinds of knots in my stomach but nothing like I used to feel.

Raising little ones can feel this way. The younger the child, the more anxious a mom can feel. You can't catch your breath even for a minute when they are one and just start walking or during the 'terrible twos' when they think the antique lamp your grandmother gave you is their new toy. You get my point. As our children get older, we are still driving them around, balancing schedules, and making sure their needs are being met. I don't know if that ever really stops until they are out of our homes, and even then we are still going to worry about our children.

Let's break this down into sections, starting with **sleep.**

Get better sleep.

Sleep has to be one of the most important things we need to do for our bodies and minds to keep us healthy. It's hard to get restful sleep when we have little ones who come into our bedroom at night to wake us, want to get in bed with us, or get up at the crack of dawn.

One of my daughters used to wake me up nearly every night and the next day I would walk around in a fog, my eyes puffy and swollen. I didn't feel good on either the inside or the outside. How can you feel good when you aren't getting proper sleep? So, I started giving them little prizes for staying in their beds all night. Hey, bribery works with kids and at certain ages you have to do what you must.

I now have two tablets for each of my daughters, and some mornings I do let them play with them while I get a little extra sleep. Do I feel I am a bad mom for letting them play on their tablets early in the morning so I can get a little extra sleep on days they don't have school? NO! I can tell you I would be much worse if I were tired all day and didn't get enough good rest. To get those extra winks, do what you can to be able to get proper sleep. If letting your child sleep with you works for you, then great. But if lack of sleep is affecting you negatively, then get a good game plan together on how to get your little one to stay in bed. Yes, bribery works!

Also, a good bedtime routine at night is key. Try to go to sleep around the same time every night within the hour. Relax before you go to bed. Research shows you get a better night's sleep when you wind down 30-60 minutes before you are ready for bed.

TV isn't good for you right before bed, but reading, meditating, journaling, bubble baths, and sex, if you're partnered, are some better methods to relax before bedtime. Try to establish a good bedtime routine. If you have lunches to pack or things to do in the morning, get into the habits of doing some of these things the night before. That way when you are in bed trying to sleep, your mind isn't thinking of what you still need to do. This will help you get a better night sleep and if you're running a little behind in the morning, you won't be in a panic.

Nights should be dedicated to winding down, having a little time for yourself or for you and your partner. Do not keep running from the time you put your children to bed to the time you go to sleep. It's good to have some time for yourself at night, but don't stay up later than you should because you feel that's your only quiet time. Staying up late can have a negative effect because you're depriving yourself of that extra hour that can make a big difference in your life the next day.

To pave the way for better sleep, follow these simple, yet effective, sleep tips:

- Stick to a sleep schedule, even on weekends.
- Practice a relaxing bedtime ritual.
- Exercise daily (no exercise 60-80 minutes before bedtime).
- Evaluate your bedroom for comfort, temperature, lighting, etc.
- Sleep on a comfortable mattress and pillow.
- Turn off all electronics before bed.

Most importantly, *make sleep a priority.* You must schedule sleep like any other daily activity, so put it on your "to-do list" and cross it off every night. But don't make it the thing you do only after everything else is done. Stop doing other things so you get the sleep you need.

If you can't always get a full night of sleep on weekdays and don't have time during the day for naps, then perhaps your spouse could get up with the kids while you sleep in or just lie in bed so you can ease into your morning. One day a week you can catch up. You can catch up on sleep while your child(ren) are with their dad. If they don't go with their dad, ask a family member, friend, or neighbor. That's what I used to do.

Learn to say NO.

Don't get involved in every activity there is. If you honestly don't want to do something, but instead you do it out of embarrassment of saying no, or out of a sense of obligation, then you will be miserable doing that thing. Face it, there are things in this life we don't want to do, but we know we have to do them, we know we can't say no, and we don't have a choice. But when it's things we *can* say no to, and are not just because we feel put on the spot or obligated, then we are doing ourselves an injustice.

If you say YES to what makes you happy and to the things you are drawn to and feel passionate about, watch how much happier and less stressed you will be.

Recently I had my eyes opened to something I've been doing. I would get text messages from longtime friends inviting me to get together to have coffee or lunch. I was accepting these invitations despite having little free time. I would meet with these old friends and the whole time I was wishing I would have filled my day with things more meaningful to me. I did enjoy my time with these ladies, but I discovered that I've grown apart from them and I was only saying yes so I wouldn't hurt their feelings. The truth is I wasn't pleasing me, I was saying yes to make them happy, while I was wishing I could be doing something else to make me happy. Then, when I would pick up my daughters from school, I resented how I spent my free time. I wasn't refilling my cup—I wasn't wisely using my time the way I would have liked. Now I try to use my free time in a way that's more satisfying to me, and I must say, I've been a lot happier.

Yes, it's important to go to all of your kids' games and extra activities if you can. Kids don't forget mom and dad cheering them on from the stands. That means the world to them and brings joy to their hearts. However, ask yourself: Do you need to be the head of the PTA and volunteer at every school function just to check a box or so that Miss Suzie Q thinks you're a great mom? I can tell you the answer NO. Your children will love you regardless and will know you are there for them. Be there for them when they need you, not to impress Miss Suzie Q or the Joneses at a school function.

It's also OK to say NO you cannot work that extra day or can't cover a coworker this weekend. Remember, you matter; your life and your time are just as important as the next person's.

Simplify your life.

Simplifying your home helps you simplify your life. Must you have a home where visitors can come in and eat off your floor? No! If you put that kind of pressure on yourself, you add unnecessary stress to your life. We are here to de-stress, and getting rid of clutter inside your home and keeping it out will help your mental state and lower your stress levels.

Clutter in the home comes from not having a designated area for each item. So, start now with declaring designated areas for your things and your kids' things. My daughters and I now have a coat rack, hat box, and shoe box near a specific door where they take off their coats, shoes, and hats. That alone reduced stress and mess in what is now my mudroom.

I have also put their toys in boxes and organized their play area, so at the end of the day it's easier for them to clean up. The bonus is they are learning to be more organized in the process. It's been a win-win in my home for all three of us.

If you study the lives of successful, productive people, you will notice two common habits: they follow strict routines on a daily basis, and they try to keep their space as organized as possible, whether it's their living space, office space, or their personal retreat.

Organization is key to a less stressful existence. A messy space adds stress and will diminish productivity. Go through your home space, office space, basement, etc., and start de-cluttering. If there's something you haven't used in years, get rid of it. Trash it, sell it, or give it away. Rarely will you ever need it later. Don't buy or accept things from other people that you won't use but think perhaps you will use *someday*. It's not likely you'll use it… ever.

If you need help organizing, don't be afraid to ask for help. Also, I know women, myself included, who have hired cleaning ladies. If you're a stay-at-home mom who feels she can't keep up, hire people to help you organize. Not everyone can afford to hire a professional organizer, but if you need help keeping up on weekly cleaning and have the extra funds to hire someone, do it. That's one less thing on your to do list, and you will come home to a fresh, clean house. Or split chores with your spouse. There's no reason to handle it all by yourself. You are only one person, not some super heroine.

Create some privacy.

Have a space in your home that is reserved only for you, a place you can go to reflect, journal, meditate, and read. This will be a space to catch your breath on days you need it. If you're like me, you may need to retreat there every day, if only for a few minutes. For me, this space is my bedroom. By creating your own physical retreat in your home, you will have a place that creates a mental space where you can go to shut down your mind's clutter.

Slow down.

Slowing down can be tough, especially for someone like me. Because I have so much excess energy at times, I find slowing down very difficult.

Despite our efforts as women, we can't always be at our best. We aren't always feeling our best, either. Get to know your body clock—when to work diligently and when to take time to relax. Our bodies will tell us. In fact, sometimes our bodies scream at us. That's when you know you are at your worn-out point.

Decluttering isn't only about removing material things from your life, it's also about clearing your mental clutter. Maintain regular mental decluttering by letting go of hatred, bitterness, and worry. Doing this may help you enjoy life more. You can remove these emotions through daily journaling and through meditation, which we'll get into later. If a thought or emotion is keeping you from performing well or becoming a better person, get rid of it.

Having a to-do list will help you slow down if you don't deviate from the list in a day, but also allow yourself some leeway if you don't accomplish everything on your list. Some people create a not-to-do list to keep themselves from working nonstop all day. Do whatever works for you, but lists do help you stay on task and keep you from ruminating on negative things. This creates more mental space to allow you to slow down and take in more of life's good things. As you drive to work, take time to notice the beautiful, fallen snow that makes the ground look untouched, or those spring flowers starting to bloom, or the smile on your child's face when they make you proud. Each day notice a few ordinary things that become extraordinary when you take the time to notice.

Deep breathing also helps a lot with slowing down. The beauty of deep breathing is that it can be done anywhere: driving, playing with your child(red), sitting at your desk, or walking.

Just breathe.

Our brains are wired to fight, flight, or freeze. When we are now faced with something new or stressful, we often respond by increasing that stress. We hold our breath, which overstimulates our brains, and that's when we don't make the best decisions. Think about when we're scared or even just learning something new. During those times, we often hold our breath the entire time, which makes us even more anxious. Instead, if we just breathed, our whole body could relax, allowing our body to be more still.

Staying present.

Part of why we often have a hard time slowing down or reducing our stress is we are trying to pay attention to too many things. We are overstimulated these days between social media and information overload. We don't slow down long enough to actually see what's in front of us, raising our stress levels even more because we don't know which way to move forward. If we just pause and focus on one area, we might see that we are less anxious, can think more clearly, and actually experience a deep sense of joy.

Meditate.

One of my favorites: meditation. Meditation and daily prayer have many health benefits. Before I started meditating, I would wake up feeling anxious every day. It was not a comfortable feeling. In a later chapter, I will write about living spiritually so I will go deeper about meditation, prayer, and spirituality then. For now, I want to talk about meditation because it's one of the best ways to a deep sense of peace. I believe wholeheartedly in meditation as a relief for stress. I even went through a teacher training program and got certified to teach it to others.

Having a routine of some kind, whether it is meditation or prayer, is a great way to help your mind and body relax and reconnect. It's also a good technique for letting go of things and giving them to God. Without a Higher Being or consciousness to turn to, you are left to struggle alone. You need a let-go outlet.

My let-go outlet is God. When I am struggling, I write Him letters. I pray to Him to take away burdens I am carrying or to give me additional strength to carry them. I can't say how many times I would have possibly had a serious meltdown if I didn't have a Higher Being to turn to. We need faith in a spirit or higher power to help us carry the load.

I use the terms God and meditation separately, but some use them together. I use meditation to calm and relax my whole being and listen. I have found many answers and guidance come up when you are meditating in stillness.

I wake up every morning and I do a morning, guided, grounding meditation or a positive morning affirmation meditation. I meditate for about 10-20 minutes and it starts my day in a positive direction. Meditation and prayer have made me more ready to face my day, whether it's good, bad, or indifferent.

Once in a while, I also do a night meditation to help me sleep. Yoga nidra (yogic sleep) night meditation really works wonders! As I said, God gives me the desire to meditate. I know this because at a rough time I prayed to Him to show me how to help myself on how to lighten my load and enjoy life more. Sure enough, I stumbled upon a guided meditation that helped me. Since then, I have become a great advocate and believer in meditation. I meditate every day and I pray to God every day. The one thing I also do every night before bed is to make sure I thank God for everything I feel gratitude for in my life. Doing a gratitude prayer every night in silence, and with my children, has worked wonders in my life.

People also use yoga as a way to get in touch with their spiritual side. I always feel I leave my yoga class with a clear mind and strong body. I feel as though I leave behind all the baggage I may have carried in to the class with me. Yoga is a great practice that lets us get in touch with our inner source or higher power. Having an inner connection to self or higher power is healing and helps deal with everyday challenges. We all have difficulties and need support to help us through them.

CHALLENGE: Write down on a sheet of paper the activities that do and don't serve you any longer. Do yourself a favor: Start saying no to those things you list that don't serve you any longer.

CHALLENGE: Pick one room, closet, or drawer in your home that you are going to declutter.

STANDING GROUNDING MEDITATION

Set a timer for 5-7 minutes.
Stand up slowly…
Bend your knees slightly with your feet planted on the ground.
Take a moment to feel your center (between your rib cage and pelvic area).

Imagine your feet have roots that are planted deep into the ground.
Breathe in for 3.
Breathe out for 5.
Repeat: *I am standing in my inner power.*
I am Centered.
I am Strong.
I am Grounded.
Keep breathing and repeating the mantras until your time is up.

PROGRESSIVE MUSCLE RELAXATION MEDITATION

Consult with your doctor if you have a history of muscle spasms and or an illness that may be aggravated by tensing muscles.

Take a few minutes to breathe in and out in slow, deep breaths.

Shift your attention to your right foot, tensing the muscles, squeezing as tightly as you can. Hold for a count of 10. Imagine your right foot becoming relaxed and limp. Then over to the left foot, follow the same sequence of muscle tension and release

Right calf, then left calf.
Right thigh, then left thigh.
Squeeze and release tension in butt and hips.
Suck in the stomach, breathe in, breath out, and release.
Chest.
Back.
Right arm, then left arm.
Right hand, then left hand.
Neck and Shoulders.
Face.

Between each body part, breathe in and exhale. Try to stay in a relaxed state. This will take practice at first but soon enough your body will feel more relaxed.

Chapter 3

STEP 3: FINDING BALANCE

Are you temporarily out of balance?

Finding balance in life is a challenge for us all. The one thing we wish for is more time. Even people I know who don't have children still find it challenging to create a good balance for their lives. When you have a balance for your life you become a happier and more peaceful person. What is important and how much time we spend on certain factors is always in flux.

Having good balance in our lives is more about being present with each thing we are doing and giving it our full attention. It's learning to compartmentalize your life and being present for the compartment you are in at the moment. If we aren't present, we can't enjoy or concentrate on what we are doing.

Happiness isn't a destination but a way of living. Change doesn't happen overnight, but you can start now by living life with a better balance. The younger your children are, the more likely they are to drain your energy. Our jobs can also drain us so make sure you are filling your own cup. You must add "me-time" into the equation. While men may have their Man Caves, women should have their Sacred Spaces. To create better balance in your life, make sure you ask for help when you need it. We moms often don't want to ask for help, but it's necessary. You are only one person; you need a good network of people to help you. Don't be embarrassed or see it as a sign of weakness. Remember, it takes a village to raise a child, and most of us have more than one child, so it may take two villages.

I've realized that if I focus on smaller goals in various areas of my life, I'll feel more satisfied than focusing solely on one area of my life. Are we ever going to find a perfect balance in our lives? Probably not, but it rarely makes sense to hyper-focus on only one thing.

For me the biggest piece of pie right now is my children. Most likely, that's how it will be for most of us during the child-raising years. However, I noticed when I wasn't giving myself much of a life beyond my little girls, I felt more stressed and unhappy, and didn't have as much to give them because I wasn't doing other things to fulfill my life and make me happy. I still struggle with balance, despite not having a husband to contend with, but then I don't have his help as some married moms do. So I guess that's a balance of sorts, too.

Balance is a sought-after thing for us all. Did you know that a Google search of "How to find balance in your life" brings up 332,000,000 results!? While I am no expert on balance, being a Creative Coach, Meditation Instructor, and someone who concentrates on living and teaching mindfulness, I will do my best to share what I know about to find better balance in our lives.

Keep in mind that balance is not a final goal but rather an ongoing process. Rather than trying to stay balanced, think of yourself as practicing balancing, over and over again. Like yoga, it's a practice. You keep practicing. It's the same with balance. It's not a destination—it's something that's constantly shifting and changing so the best thing to do is approach it day by day. Let's not be hard on ourselves when we get out of balance but simply try to put ourselves back behind the wheel.

Another important factor is to prioritize our goals, deciding which ones are more important, and then doing the most important ones first. To stay on course you may have to reexamine your priorities often. Once you make a decision on what is important, focus on it and get it done. Be specific. It's more useful to say, "I'm going to spend an hour alone with each child on Wednesday this week," than to say, "I'm going to have quality time with each of my children." Set something specific. If it's vague, it will be hard to recognize whether or not you've accomplished that goal, which, in turn, makes it hard to feel in balance. I can't say this enough: Ask for help. You must have someone else help you with things, or you will burn out. It's extremely hard to find good balance in your life if you don't get help with child care, work, or household chores.

None of us really knows how well we are doing with change in our lives unless we are willing to reassess our position. Don't feel that your decisions are made in concrete; if something feels that it isn't working, be willing to look at a new decision. Most importantly, make time for yourself every day.

When we don't have a good balance in our lives, it can make us anxious or depressed. When we are raising our children but not setting any personal goals for ourselves, or having quiet time, or pampering ourselves, we can start to feel as though our lives are less meaningful. You will lose connection with the most important person in your life, YOU.

We love our children more than life itself, but someday our kids are going to find their own friends, or leave us to go on their own adventures. Yes, right now it's our job to take care of them, love them, and spend beautiful, quality time with them making memories, but you still need to have your own life besides raising your family.

You may not have many career goals, or your goal may be to do yoga, or go to the spa once in a while, or have some alone time. Whatever your goal, big or small, you must have other things to focus on beyond your children. My kids come first, and they always will, but I enjoy and appreciate them more when I accomplish other goals in my life.

My two daughters look up to me, so I want them to see a strong capable woman who loves them, puts them first, tries to be the best mommy she can be, but also has other things going in her life. I want them to see me as accomplished. I want my daughters someday to be capable, have a family, and also have a life for themselves where they pursue personal goals. These strengths can be passed on from generation to generation.

I was raised in a very traditional Italian culture. My mom focused on taking care of her children as well as taking care of her parents. She learned from her mother that the only thing that was important was raising your kids, cooking, keeping a clean house, and constantly meeting others' needs. Those women should be nominated for sainthood because many were suffering inside with depression and feelings of unworthiness, but that is all they knew. The point I want to make is that by achieving a better balance in our lives, we are teaching our kids a better way to live.

CHALLENGE: Complete the Wheel of Life exercise below.

Your Wheel of Life!

Friends & Family

Love Life

Personal Growth

Health

0   10

Money

Fun & Leisure

Career

Home Environment

Complete the Wheel:
1. Review the 8 Wheel Categories - think briefly what a satisfying life might look like for you in each area.
2. Next, draw a line across each segment that represents your satisfaction score for each area.
   • Imagine the center of the wheel is 0 and the outer edge is 10
   • Choose a value between 1 (very dissatisfied) and 10 (fully satisfied)
   • Now draw a line across each wheel group (where your chosen value would fall) and write the score alongside it.
IMPORTANT: Use the FIRST number (score) that pops into your head, not the number you think it *should* be!

Follow us on Facebook to get updates: SinglemomlifeErie PA

MEDITATION FOR BALANCE

Find a comfortable place to sit. You do not have to sit cross-legged. The best time to do a balancing meditation is in the morning upon awakening or right before bed to release excess energy to help you get a good night's sleep.

Choose your mantra. A mantra is a word or phrase that you focus on and repeat to yourself during meditation. Since we are learning how to have better balance, the best words or phrases to use are:

I am balanced, I release excess energy.

I am present. Today I will be focused and present in all I do.

My life is in perfect harmony and balance.

Close your eyes and begin taking some deep breaths. Inhale slowly through your nose and exhale out of your mouth. Three breaths in and five breaths out.

Begin repeating your mantra.

Stop repeating the mantra. After approximately 10-15 minutes, you may stop repeating your mantra and continue sitting with your eyes softened and gently closed. Relax in stillness. This will help you create space in your mind and relax your body.

If you find that 20 minutes is too long for you, start small and slowly add more time as you get comfortable with this practice.

For meditation to be truly effective on your mind, body, and soul, it must be practiced daily.

Chapter 4

STEP 4: I AM LOVE

"Loving yourself isn't vanity; it is sanity."—Katrina Mayer

I think loving oneself is one of the hardest things to accomplish. Nobody taught me how to take time for myself. When I first became a mom I felt I had to be always doing something or I wasn't being productive enough. My mom was the same way. She always had to be doing something and never took time for her own self-care. When I became a mom, the only thing I knew was the way my mom did it. That was ingrained in me.

As time went on, I started to experience anxiety and depression. I realized I was neglecting myself. Then the worrisome thought came to my mind that if I am not OK, how is my daughter going to be OK? At that time, I had only one daughter. Slowly I started pulling myself out of my depression and anxiety with a little self-care. I did this through meditation, prayer, asking my parents for help with child care since I was struggling, and getting a babysitter occasionally even if I could just go to my room to read or lie down for a little bit.

With each day and as my daughters are growing, I am learning how to take better care of myself. Someday when they are mothers and bring their own babies home from the hospital, I hope they will be better equipped to take care of themselves to be the best mommies they can be to their children.

Let's dive into this self-love business more deeply, dissect it, and learn new ways to take care of ourselves, appreciate ourselves, and love ourselves so we can be the best examples for our children. I will start with this Bible verse about love and how we can relate it to ourselves. I believe it's not only about loving other people, but loving ourselves as well. How can we truly love others if we don't love ourselves? I mean loving ourselves in a healthy way so we are better for other people, not in an egotistical or narcissistic way.

You may be familiar with the Bible verse, "Love is patient, love is kind," from 1 Corinthians 13, 4-8, (New International Version).

Love is patient.

Be patient with yourself when you are having a problem or struggling with something within yourself. Know it will get better. Also know you are not perfect, so be gentle with yourself.

Love is kind.

How kind are you to yourself? Do you do nice things for yourself? Buy yourself some flowers, take a walk, or take a bubble bath. The list is endless. When was the last time you were kind to yourself?

Love does not envy.

When you are watching what everyone else is doing, do you compare yourself to them? That's one way to get down on yourself very quickly. Try to be the best you can be for yourself and your kids. The person you see at school or your neighbor that you may compare yourself to as a mother is also struggling in her own way. What we perceive isn't always the reality of a situation.

Make a pact now to stop comparing, and promise to be your best. Be happy being you!

Love does not boast.

Bragging to make yourself feel better, or putting someone else down, reflects a false sense of who you are. When you brag, you aren't standing in your true power; you are actually feeling intimidated or insecure with the person you are conversing with. Bragging isn't a form of self-love. Bragging actually comes from a place of fear that you are not enough on your own. I am here to tell you, you are enough!

Love is not proud.

It is good to be proud of your accomplishments. You should be proud! However, to feel your worth only through your accomplishments isn't self-love. Instead it's feeling unworthy unless you are doing something worthwhile. Know when God created us, He created all of us in His image, regardless of what we accomplish in this life. Remember, your life is as valuable as the next person's regardless of accomplishments.

Be proud in an authentic way. Be proud you were created in God's image, and be proud when you help people in an authentic way, not wanting or asking for anything in return.

Love is not self-seeking.

Self-seeking is different from self-love. Self-seeking behaviors are seeking out *things* that may give us pleasure that aren't necessarily good for us—like alcohol, drugs, sex, gambling, going from one romantic relationship to the next, and not giving ourselves enough time to let our wounds properly heal.

Self-seeking behaviors try to fill a void with unhealthy behaviors. It's better to choose behaviors that fill your soul, that put you in line with feeling better about who you are, and in turn, make you a better and more fulfilled mom, friend, daughter, co-worker, and all around human being.

Volunteering is also a form of self-love so long as you are volunteering for the right reasons and don't put yourself in burnout mode by volunteering. Helping other humans makes us learn new things about ourselves and feel good about who we are. Community helps build self-love as well.

Love is not easily angered.

You are human. You make mistakes. That's OK. Again, be gentle with yourself. Learn to forgive yourself. Do not beat yourself up over mistakes you may have made. We are human. We all make mistakes. Learn from those mistakes and move on. Do not beat yourself up over them.

Love keeps no record of wrongs.

Don't tally up all your past wrongs or mistakes. That's not self-love; that's a form of self-hatred. I'll bet you forgive others and look past their mistakes more than you overlook your own. Well, that shouldn't be. Forgive yourself as well. Know you are learning and growing every day and you are no longer the same person you were yesterday. When you have learned the lesson, let the mistake go.

Love does not delight in evil.

Participating in gossip to help ourselves feel better isn't self-love. That gives us a temporary high so we don't have to look deep within ourselves to see what it is that we are lacking.

Love rejoices in the truth.

Rejoice in being who you are. Be true to yourself about your likes and dislikes. Being not afraid to speak your truth is a form of self-love. The more you stand in your truth about who you really are, the better you will feel about yourself. Also, your children are watching you and learning how to be themselves through your behavior. It's a well-known fact that once you really become yourself and stand in that power, you start attracting better things and better people into your life.

Love always protects.

Self-preservation. Ladies, protecting yourself is a beautiful act of self-love. If, like me, you are a single mom in the dating world, you need to be careful whom you choose to bring into your home. I have dated only one guy since my divorce and he didn't meet my children until the 6-month mark.

I am learning to protect my heart and share it only with people who seem to be genuine and have good motives. I used to be the kind of person who would fall in love, get swept away and fall in love with love. That wasn't self-love; that was me caught up in some self-seeking fantasy. I would fall in love with a man's *potential*.

A good tip I learned is to be mindfully optimistic, and don't rush in with the heart. Make sure you are also using logic. The head and heart must find their balance. If the scales are tipped, a disaster could happen. For you married women, protection isn't only about romantic love. You need to protect yourself from people in your life that you know are there for the wrong reasons and never really showed their genuine love for you or who take advantage of you. If everything has to be their way, those aren't people you want in your circle. So, part of self-love is protecting yourself and keeping the good and weeding out the not so good. Don't let people take advantage of you. You deserve much better than that. Remember, people will treat you as you allow them to treat you.

Love always trusts.

Trust in yourself and listen to your instincts. They say a woman's intuition will not lead her wrong. I used to struggle with this, big time. I didn't have a lot of self-trust within myself so I am one to always ask other people's opinions, which is OK sometimes. But part of loving yourself is trusting yourself. We trust other people, so why not trust ourselves?

Love always hopes.

It doesn't matter what we have going on in our lives, there is always something to be grateful or hopeful about. It's difficult to hope in times of despair, but holding on to hope is a form of self-love. Holding on to hope has pulled many people out of deep depressions. Being hopeless has made many people depressed. When you feel sad, always do a self-check and see if you aren't feeling hopeful. Chances are that will be part, if not all, of the problem. Find time to journal, which is beautiful for the soul anyway, and during your journaling always end with something you are grateful and hopeful for. It might seem challenging in the beginning, but after some time it will become second nature to you.

Love always perseveres.

Love doesn't give up. Don't give up on you, your dreams, and your family. Know whatever happens, you will be OK. Say it to yourself right now: I am OK! Now that you're a mom, your dreams may take a little longer to happen, but don't give up on them. I promise, with determination, you will get there. Never give up on YOU! You are special. You aren't the kind of woman anyone should give up on, and you are the kind of woman who deserves to persevere!

Love never fails.

True love doesn't fail you… so don't fail yourself. Learn to count on yourself for love when you need it. It's good to have other people in your life who love you, but you also need to love and appreciate yourself fully if you want other people to truly love you. The love we give ourselves is a love that stays with us forever and helps us make better choices in life and be better mommies to our children.

Know thyself.

- Acknowledge your thoughts and feelings, your fears, and fantasies.
- Spend some quality time alone.
- Turn off the computer, the phone, and the TV.
- Put on your favorite music or simply savor the silence.
- Entertain a program of non-directed self-discovery.
- Clear your mind of inner chatter and let it wander where it will. Focus on *being* rather than doing.
- Ask yourself personal questions. Interview yourself.
- Buy a book on self-discovery. Have fun reconnecting with yourself when you have some extra time. You never know what you may discover.
- Try new things to learn more about your likes and dislikes.

Take an interest in yourself.

- Engage in projects of self-expression in order to reconnect with your higher nature and your inner best self.
- Go for a run, walk, swim, or bike ride.
- Practice yoga. Meditate. Drum, chant, or dance.

- Write in your journal.
- Create an altar with things that are meaningful to you.
- Do things that make you laugh.

Don't be afraid to pay yourself a compliment. Try to say something nice about yourself every day. Mother yourself just as you mother your children. Build yourself up. This is even a bigger bonus if your children hear you talk this way to yourself because research shows kids learn a lot of their own self-talk and inner dialogue from their parents or caregivers.

Maintaining a personal journal is an excellent way to practice self-love. A special place to share your thoughts and feelings, a journal provides you with a place to vent, confess, and express yourself in any way. The process of writing down your experiences can be exhilarating!

Saying affirmations is the use of positive self-statements to help you transform your thoughts. I use affirmations daily and they have helped me build more confidence and self-trust.

Meditation and prayer are lovely ways to listen and set yourself on the right path. Prayer helps me pull from my inner strength, while meditation really helps to center me and clear my mind. For me, these two things in combination are extremely life-changing and powerful.

Self-love can come in the form of meaningful relationships with others who understand and get you, whatever you call them: your tribe, your people. When you take time to nurture those relationships, you are building interpersonal skills and learning more about yourself. Research shows the happiest people on the planet are people who feel they are involved in a community. If you don't have a good group to belong to or don't have many friends, start your own group. You can create a moms' group or a group that has to do with something you may be passionate about. I created a group for single moms called "Single Mom Life." We meet monthly in person. I recently created a private Facebook group called Single Mom Life. Please feel free to connect with us.

Be mindful of what you feed your mind, body, and soul. Pay less attention to what you see on social media, television, movies, and promotional ads.

It's all how we want to live our lives, but the worst thing you can do for yourself is pick yourself apart. The best thing you can do for yourself is embrace how God made you. It's great to exercise, get facials, and drink lots of water, but when you start feeling you're not skinny enough, not pretty enough, and not rich enough, you are running away from happiness and fulfillment, not toward them. Look in the mirror. Praise yourself. Write down ten of your best physical features. We all have flaws and we can be our own worst critics. I have been around some beautiful people who think they are ugly. It's so sad when you see women do this to themselves.

Improving our parenting means gaining a better understanding of ourselves. All parents both love and hate themselves, and they extend both of these reactions to their children. Because our kids come from us, we often confuse our own self-perceptions and experiences with theirs. When parents feel good about themselves, they are much better able to extend this positive sense of self to their children. They can engage in activities, relate to, and offer their children support from a place of confidence and ease.

It is important to be aware of the example we set for our children. What we say to them, what we say about them, and what we say about ourselves will have a profound influence on how they view themselves. The more attuned we are to ourselves, the better able we are to react sensitively to our children. The healthier we are emotionally, the less likely we are to project our own negative experiences and self-critical thoughts onto our kids.

Perfection is impossible. But self-reflection helps us do better as parents. The more honest, open, and mindful we make the environment we share with our children, the more we enable our children to be resilient and to move confidently and independently into the world.

Self-love starts with you. If you want your children to grow up in a home with a happy mama, start your self-love journey today. You will feel, act, and look better! I am counting on you to do this. Teach your kids the true meaning of self-love and care as they grow. They will then be ahead of where you and I were at their age, and this is a gift that will keep on giving from generation to generation.

When you aren't practicing self-love, you are actually practicing the opposite, which leads to anxiety, depression, burnout, and low self-esteem. Don't feel bad; most of us weren't taught self-love, but we have the chance to change that and help make the world a better place.

CHALLENGE: Make a list of all of your good qualities. If you get stumped, imagine someone you love naming the top three best qualities that they love about you. Next time you criticize yourself, take out your piece of paper and read all of your good qualities. At some point you will not be needing that piece of paper. You will be able to say and think of your best qualities in your head to counterbalance the negative ones.

CHALLENGE: What you tell yourself first thing in the morning will help determine your experience for the rest of the day. Wake up every day for the next 21 days and the minute you open your eyes say something positive about yourself. Do the same exercise before you go to bed.

SELF-LOVE MEDITATION

Close your eyes.

Breathe in and out slowly.

Let all of your thoughts float by like clouds floating in the sky.

Imagine floating on a raft in a calming river, a warm sun beating down on your beautiful face and body.

Imagine letting go and floating in the river of self-love.

This river is creating new loving energy throughout your entire body.

You are growing and changing just like the river. You are not the same person you were yesterday or five minutes ago.

You are emerging into a beautiful butterfly; your colors are becoming more vibrant.

Now use whatever mantra you feel most comfortable with:

I am Nature's Miracle.

I am unique and loved for who I am.

God made me perfectly in His image.

A snowflake never falls in the wrong place; I am where I am meant to be.

Close this meditation by ending with your name and a word of kindness to yourself.

Chapter 5

STEP 5: GRATEFUL LIVING

Gratitude is a skill we must teach ourselves. It is something I am starting to teach my two daughters, who are four and six. I have my daughters each name three things for which they are grateful. My six year old loves this exercise and completely gets it; my four year old, not so much. She will say, "Mommy, I am grateful for my bedroom window, my teeth, and the door in my room." It makes me laugh every time because you never know what will come out of this innocent child's mouth. But I don't mind. I hope I am creating the habit of gratitude that will carry with them through a lifetime.

Let's try to be grateful, not only in moments of weakness, when we are down, or in moments of victory, but also in our everyday lives. I started a nightly ritual where I journal three things I am grateful for, and in the morning when I wake up, I write down another three things I am grateful for. This keeps me positively focused and helps me see the little blessings every day that, without doing this exercise, I could have easily missed.

Just recently I suffered some anxiety and mild depression. Whether you are a single mom or a married mom, we all struggle on some level. I was feeling sorry for myself and felt this old hurt and anger I had inside me. Generally, I am a positive person—sometimes too positive. I have been told that I wear rose-colored glasses, but now I was feeling all these intense negative emotions. I wondered how to deal with these crazy feelings that were knocking at my door and wouldn't go away. I was overwhelmed with sadness, anger, and grief. In the past I would have talked myself out of these emotions, but instead of running or fighting them, I accepted, faced them, sat with them, and let them overwhelm me some days.

I wasn't passive in this process. I talked back to these emotions. I could feel this old pain and perhaps some new pain leaving my body. Literally a miracle was happening. It was incredible. I felt free. I felt rejuvenated. And I felt strong.

I didn't push these emotions back down inside, nor did I try and talk myself out of them. I let them be. I felt like a new person in the making. Ever since that moment, I have been more grateful than I ever have been in my whole life. That moment taught me this: the more you can sit with your own pain and the shadows that live inside us—the light, the dark, the good, the bad, and the downright ugly—the more you can *also* sit with your joy and the many blessings that are bestowed on you as well.

If you aren't comfortable with sadness, loneliness, and those other tough emotions, you won't be as comfortable with the joyous emotions either. You will always feel unbalanced and off-kilter. It's when we acknowledge what we are feeling that we can find our true inner balance. I used to think only people with terrible lives get depressed, or that something must be wrong. Feeling overly anxious and getting weird thoughts can happen to us all. Most of the time it is not clinical, but rather is because we aren't facing something we should be facing, whether it is our emotions or a real problem we are battling within our lives. See your doctor if you find yourself severely depressed or anxious. But, even if you are getting medical treatment for depression or anxiety, having a daily ritual of setting aside time to say, think, or write what you are grateful for can work wonders in your life.

There are some days I don't just yell at my kids, I scream at them. I'm ashamed to admit this, but sometimes it's the reality of my situation. I recognize most of the time when I react like this, it's because of my own issues and not the way my daughters are behaving. If I healed every part of myself and dealt with all my issues, would that make my daughters listen and hang on to every word I say? No, but it would make the way I deal with them and discipline them different.

Most of the time, we react to what we are feeling on the inside. No matter how good you feel on the inside, some days will not be perfect nor will you have a method to deal with your kids down to a science. But you will be happier, they will be happier, and your home will have good vibes running through it… if you stop in those moments before you lose it and think of at least one thing you are grateful for. Or you tell yourself in those moments of craziness, *I accept this moment as is. I am a good mother, my kids love me, I love them and this moment isn't going to last. We will be OK.* Try it. You will slowly notice that you can deal with the ups and downs of parenthood with a little more grace.

If you daily include something you are grateful for about each of your kids, whether it's something special you share between the two of you, or something unique and special about their personality, I guarantee you will slowly start to develop a better relationship with each one of your children. And when times get tough, those warm thoughts about them will flood your mind and heart and help you connect with them on a deeper level. Before long, you will be having fewer battles.

What our children really want is our love, our time, and most of all, our attention; and they will take it any way they can get it. Someday you will look back and think of the rough moments you are going through now and be grateful for many of them. I find myself doing that now. Sometimes I find myself laughing about some of the past "bad" stuff, like my daughter, Abriana, revenge-peeing on my floor because she was mad at me or her sister. I laugh now—and think, *What a stinker!* But how clever she was at 2 years old to know that would trip my trigger. At the time I was furious. I'm not saying we should rejoice or act to our kids as though it's OK when they do something bad, but rather, we should learn to appreciate each moment for what it is.

Sometimes it is a great teaching moment for your child or it may be a teaching moment for you to learn more patience, to learn to control your temper, or learn to face your anger, or your ways of dealing with your anger. In the next chapter, we'll see how our kids can be our greatest teachers. Most moments are not life or death, and when we react as if they are, we forget how to be grateful for some of the gifts that our bestowed upon us. Someday, when we look back, we will be grateful for these moments, so why steal the joy of the moment? Be GRATEFUL now.

I read something interesting the other day and have been exploring this theory in my personal life: **Nobody can be grateful and fearful at the same time.** Test this theory for yourself.

When we yell at or are mad at our children, many times it is because we are either scared or sad. Also, when we are angry, it is either because we are scared or sad. Anger is a second emotion, not a first one.

As mothers, we provide the environment in which our kids can flourish and grow up as self-sufficient, confident adults. In our society, that isn't always easy. It starts with our mental attitude, the way we live our lives, and the rituals we adopt. They are more likely to follow or choose their own at some point, but they will somewhat mimic what felt comfortable to them as children, things they saw their parents do. My kids already know things about God and how to pray. I am building a strong faith foundation for them at a young age.

Rather than wait until I am down, I use gratitude and prayer in my everyday life. Every day tell your child something about them you are grateful for. Kids remember how you made them feel and remember the time you spent with them.

Something else I read long ago regarding romantic relationships was that every time you say something nice to your love interest, it is like dropping a coin in a piggy bank, but every time you say something negative, it is like taking a coin out. You hope you can deposit more coins in that bank than you withdraw. I thought we should use this same theory with our children. Just because we are the authority figures, the ones who care for them, doesn't mean we get to treat them badly or can say whatever we damn well please to them. No way. Eventually our kids will be able to choose what kind of relationship they want with us. Most likely they will base their choices on how we treated them. They may not remember the tiny details but they will remember how we made them feel most of the time. The better we feel on the inside is the better we will make them feel.

I can tell you that by being more grateful in your own life and frequently taking time to write down what you appreciate about your children will make you a happier woman and mom. You will start to see the glass as half full much more often than you see it as half empty. You will be able to sit with negative emotions more often and not run off like I once did because you will be more resilient to let go of negative emotions and not let them consume you when you have plenty of things to be grateful for.

Feeling and acting with respect and appreciation for others is perhaps the most gracious way of living. Gratitude involves letting yourself accept the gifts that come to you. We often fail to notice the countless gifts offered to us by God, nature, or whatever higher power you may believe in. Failing to notice is like refusing a gift. You are really missing out on some beautiful, miraculous experiences.

Anne Dunlea, Ph.D, recently wrote on her Grateful Parenting blog (https://gratefulness.org/blog/grateful-parenting/):

"Most parents deeply love their child, but more than a few are surprised when I ask them why they <u>like</u> their child. That's rather telling. It suggests that we parents are often not very conscious of the gifts and qualities our child has. We don't keep those in our mental awareness."

I thought this was interesting how many of us rarely take the time to get to know our child as a human being as we would a friend, instead of seeing them as: *You are the little person… I am the big person… case closed. You have to listen to me.*

Not that we should be friends with our children, but let us get to really know them as people, appreciate them for who they are. Most of us don't do this with our spouse, our friends, our parents, or worse, with ourselves. Parents appreciate their children more and are more likely to notice and reinforce what is good.

- Children feel respected and appreciated. Their gifts are noticed, which in turn bolsters confidence and self-esteem.
- Trust is strengthened on the part of both parent and child. A child who feels valued, appreciated, and respected more easily trusts her parents and accepts guidance from them. Similarly, parents feel more trust and confidence in a child they know appreciates and trusts them.

A way to gratitude for me is silencing my phone and taking some alone time to breathe and connect with God whether it's with eyes wide open or through meditation.

Acceptance. That's one word with a big meaning. To be grateful, you must accept where you are on your journey of life, and to find acceptance you must be grateful. Gratitude and acceptance go hand in hand. I don't know which one I found first, but I carry them both around with me like a necessity as important as food and water. They are my keys to bliss, balance, and contentment.

Wherever you are on this journey, my friend, you need to accept where you are. Acceptance doesn't mean being a slave to your life if you don't like the direction it is going. Acceptance also means to make a change if change is necessary, but to accept the journey as it is in the present moment. When we accept the journey as it is in the present moment, somehow peace makes its way into our hearts.

With parenting comes many different phases of our children's lives. As soon as I feel I have one of those phases figured out, another one pops up. Fortunately, phases don't last. With every bad phase my children would go through, I would feel out of control. Sometimes in my parenting, my Type A personality would emerge. What was really happening? I wasn't accepting the phase for what it was, a temporary learning experience for me and for them. Had I accepted it at the time, I would have had an easier time with it. If only I had seen the beauty in the imperfection of the moment, that is where acceptance comes in.

Even if the moment feels like hell, the first thing you should do is accept it. Picture an ocean wave coming toward you. If you try to swim against it, you will be thrown, or you will go under. That's what happens when we are not accepting life as it is at the moment.

When we learn to accept what is, that is when bright solutions start flooding our brain, or we feel a deep peace. Or we simply are able to be and find our real joy. We are teaching our children to learn acceptance. They see us accept what is, while also working toward change, if change is necessary. Remember wherever you are on the journey of life, it is all temporary. Nothing lasts; wheels are always in motion. Even if you don't want to move forward, or want things to change, things are moving and changing right now as you are reading this. Acceptance will bring you the best gift your heart can ask for: PEACE!

There is a form of therapy now called Acceptance and Commitment Therapy, or ACT. Similar to Cognitive Behavior Therapy, ACT is an action-oriented approach that helps people learn to stop avoiding, denying, and struggling with their inner emotions and, instead, accept that these deeper feelings are appropriate responses to certain situations. With this understanding, people begin to accept their issues and hardships and commit to making necessary changes in their behavior.

There is a lot of information online if you want to learn more about ACT or to find a good therapist who works with this method. If you find you have a really hard time accepting things, then it is time to maybe work with a professional who can help you sort out some of the overwhelm you may be feeling.

As mothers, the more we invest in ourselves in a positive way, the more our children will benefit from it. I hope you will invest in YOU and set aside some time each day to write down the things you are grateful for.

CHALLENGE: Make Gratitude Lists, using columns. Write things you're grateful for about yourself, your family, nature, etc. **Please** add something unique you love about each child to that list. Don't forget to write some of the unique qualities you love about yourself, or each morning, tell yourself when you look in the mirror how special you are, and pick one quality each day you love about yourself. Make sure to include things outside yourself such as beautiful flowers blooming or colorful leaves on the trees. It is very important we also pay attention to things outside of ourselves. This may seem like a lot of work, and you already have so many other things on your plate, but once you have a daily gratefulness ritual—in the morning or at night—it will not take up any more time than tooth brushing. You got this, Pretty lady!

GRATITUDE MEDITATION

Find a quiet spot. Either sit or lie down.
Breathe in and out slowly.
Inhale for three, exhale for five.
Reflect on all the people and things you are grateful for.
Repeat this 3-5 times: *All things work out for my highest good.*
Close with: *I am grateful to be here, I am worthy. I have a unique purpose to fulfill.*

When you open your eyes, smile and picture a bright white light surrounding you.

Chapter 6

STEP 6: MOTHERHOOD AS A SPIRITUAL JOURNEY

"God couldn't be everywhere, and therefore He made mothers."
—Jewish Proverb

I will start off this chapter by telling you about my crazy morning with my two daughters. I must have told them to get their shoes on 50 times and that it was time to stop coloring and get ready for school. I told them, "I was nice enough to let you girls play this morning and pull out all your art supplies." Did that comment matter to them, or make any difference, or make them get ready any faster? No, not at all, and that is when I lost it. I snapped. I wasn't just yelling at this point, I was screaming. I am ashamed to admit that and feel very guilty that they are both now away from me and at school. Luckily, I was able finally to calm myself down.

My poor six year old went to school with her eyes red from crying and my four year old was very quiet and not saying a peep in the backseat of the car on her way to school. Am I feeling some serious mom guilt about this? You bet I am.

Sometimes I can't believe it's me yelling that way at my two precious daughters. I am usually a sweet-natured, laid-back person and mother for the most part. But sometimes I lose my patience, my mind, and my cool.

I'm telling you this story because I feel motherhood is a major awakening into our own souls as human beings. The amount of things you learn about yourself when you become a mother and throughout each stage of your child's life is unbelievable. Motherhood can push us almost to the brink of insanity some days and other days have us so elated we feel one with the entire world and get a glimpse of heaven on earth. Motherhood is here to challenge us to be our best selves. Motherhood helps us see the ugliest parts of ourselves, and also the most beautiful parts of ourselves. We must honor both of these. We must honor both the light and the dark of motherhood, because there are times it is dark. Even though I try to live from my light and my God-given strength, I get on my knees and cry, beg, and pray to God. There are times of intense fear, sadness, confusion, and doubt, not to mention a hefty dose of *how-the-hell-am-I going-to-do-this?* and seemingly absolute madness.

There are also times of happy tears, joy, fun, laughter, unity, and an overwhelming sense of love. Wherever I am at the moment, I never lose the love for my children… even though some days I just want to scream my head off.

I birthed them—they are children of God. They didn't ask to be born, but, as a matter of fact, I prayed for them. I had a hard time getting pregnant with my older daughter. I remember being so sad when I would see others close to me with their children. I was happy for them, but my heart wanted to explode with desire, wanting a family of my own. However, I had no control. I just prayed and hoped it was in the cards for me, and sure enough, it was. I do appreciate my daughters. To me, being a mom is a gift that I sometimes lose sight of. I strongly feel God entrusted me enough to give me two beautiful daughters. Do I think that if someone has a hard time conceiving, or can't have children, that means God doesn't trust them to be mommies? No. I feel it just means God has other plans for them. In my experience, the journey of motherhood is a spiritual calling that we sometimes take for granted.

When you become a mother, you start living from a different level of vulnerability. It's as though, when you become a mother, you break open; your heart explodes with love, and it isn't about only you anymore. It is about caring for another human being. When you first have a child, it is all on you to keep that child alive, literally. There isn't a bigger calling or responsibility than that, wouldn't you agree?

We all will get older; it's inevitable. But will we grow up? That is up to each of us. This is where awakening comes in. It starts the moment you become a mother. For me, it started the moment I saw the two blue lines on that little stick. As mothers we're given generous doses of grace and love. We're ripped apart and broken open. We are challenged to grow up as never before. Despite the pain or struggle, the gift of parenthood cultivates our capacity to love.

Motherhood has much to teach us about our own inner world. We feel our bodies tense up, and we think are ready to lose our minds, or the eye rolling begins. I do this a lot. These are all perfect reflections of the places where I struggle, revealing where I need to grow.

When I'm struggling, it's about me, not them; it's about my unfinished business and my shortcomings. So many times I have told myself I will not yell at the kids today. If I start to lose my cool, I breathe deeply. Some days it works, and some days I bomb majorly… but, I try, and that's what's important. When I'm angry with my kids or struggling that day, I take an inventory of my inner world. It's usually something I'm struggling with on a personal level, or a negative emotion I am feeling in my body that is making me on edge with them.

Forget being around me mid-month when I am PMS-ing. When I start to see the situation in which they are driving me crazy, making me angry by not listening to me, the way I handle it is up to me. I don't have to yell and scream at them or get snappy, giving them dirty looks. That is my issue, not theirs. What triggers me may seem like it is coming from them, but much of it is coming from deep within myself.

When we have moments with our children in which we feel we are being pushed to the brink, it is time to pause and look inside ourselves. Am I saying that by healing and correcting your inner world or healing parts of yourself you will be a perfect mother? NO. But you will evolve into a better, more patient mother.

When we recognize the root of a problem, it's easier to deal with. Either we can solve the problem creatively or the problem no longer bothers us once we get to the root of it. A recurring thought I have is this: if my girls don't listen to me now, does that mean they won't listen to me *any* morning? What will it be like when they are teenagers? Of course I am going to lose it. Look how much false, anxiety-ridden stuff I put in my own head. The overgeneralization and black-and-white thinking comes from my own childhood in which one is bad or good; nothing in between.

Let me take a few breaths and use some positive reinforcement. When I change my behavior, it's as if my kids were under a magic spell because they then change their behavior, and now the ship is sailing smoothly with a calm and happy mom at the helm.

Have you ever noticed how older people are? They often become more relaxed with age. I think as time goes on, we awaken, pull back, and heal different layers of our being. It's like peeling layers of an onion. Let's not wait until our kids are out of the house to learn this. The fewer regrets we have when our kids leave the nest, the better. See this as a beautiful way to heal your inner being. What challenges you now will help you grow if you use it as a positive learning tool.

I never realized what a control freak I am until I started having kids. I would have said I was far from having Type A personality, but I learned quickly how I prefer organization, regimentation, and planning. I need to be in control. I didn't see this side of my personality until I had my first-born, Viviana.

I mention this story because either I had to learn to tone it down or I was headed for a nervous breakdown. I thought I was going to go crazy. I wanted everything just right and wanted to control everything going on. The more I needed to be in control, the more out of control I felt. For the first time in my life I learned how to *surrender*.

I thought I understood surrendering before having children. I didn't have a clue. I finally learned how to surrender and let go. My anxiety has reduced significantly. I am far more relaxed now.

This was one of the lessons and spiritual awakenings I had when I first became a mother. I surrender more and more every day. Looking back, before I started having kids, I used to suffocate life and hold on so tight to outcomes. I now give things beyond my control to God

Do I have a bedtime for my kids? Yes, but if there is a little upheaval at night and we pass our bedtime, or the meltdowns are so loud the neighbors must be needing earplugs, I let go. I surrender. I tell myself this isn't going to last forever; this is life.

When Viviana started kindergarten I was more of a mess. How will she like this new, big school? How will the kids treat her? But she is doing awesome. I worried for no reason. Again, I had to surrender to what was.

I believe surrendering is another of the many lessons motherhood teaches us. Some lessons are unique to some of us. We are each walking a different path to be our best, but some lessons of motherhood are universal.

Surrendering is one of the universal ones. If you don't learn as a mother to surrender to the higher power or the higher part of yourself, or throw it to the wind, you will have a constant inner battle and become a nervous wreck.

When I am with my daughters, I feel at home in their presence. I feel as if the whole universe is working in my favor. Being a mommy is where I belong; it's as if our three hearts beat as one big gigantic heart. Being a mom is one of my biggest callings in life. While I don't feel being a mom is my only calling, I do feel at this time in my life it is the biggest and most important one.

If, as a mom, you feel you are only existing with your child or children and don't see your purpose beyond that, then you are in for a struggle. You won't see beauty beyond chaos. You may feel your children are against you, when really they are here to teach us more about ourselves. They are here to heal us in ways we never would have imagined. We must recognize the parts of ourselves we dislike, or that seem undesirable, because they are there and they will emerge when our buttons are pushed. When we have moments of anger or resentment against our kids, that is a part of our being that is crying and calling out to be healed. Not only are we here to nurture and help our children, but they also help us as much as we help them.

When we become parents, we find a copious amount of inner strength and compassion we never knew we had. Remember in the hospital room when you looked into that sweet face before you? That tiny, helpless body and those sweet eyes that looked at you for the first time? Remember those tiny little lips that were probably kissed by an angel before we kissed them? I never felt so much love in all my life as I felt twice in the hospital as I held each of my baby girls. Your heart expanded each time you had your precious, angelic beings. Feeling this love, fear, and elation all at once isn't an accident. It is a gift. It is a calling. It is an awakening. Having children teaches us, beyond measure, so much about ourselves, our emotions, and life in general. Loving them is our spiritual practice and top priority.

Our time to impact them is now. Each day of motherhood builds on the next. Each day is a new start with not one mistake. Each day is a chance to have a do-over. Be the best parent you can, create a real home, and shower them with love, time, and understanding.

I read a great quote today: Practice being *the water and not the stone* in combative situations. My friend, Jeff, told me his father always says, "The way you treat your children when they are little is the way they will treat you when you get old."

Sometimes our best is kick-ass amazing, and some days our best is lacking, but it is always important for our children to know how much we love them. It is OK for you to let your kids see you, their mom, as a real human being. If you are having a bad day, are sad, are frustrated, or work is knocking you down, it is OK to let them know how you feel. Not that you have to give great detail, but they do need to see you as a human being, not a robot who doesn't feel bad or doesn't have bad days. The more our kids see a real person in front of them, the more authentic they will become. They will learn how to honor and communicate their feelings. With every move, we're mothering. Near and far, day and night, mothering is always in practice, full time. We know perfect parenting doesn't exist, yet we still struggle with social expectations.

Our children look to us to model how to live. They will look to us for a sense of spiritual direction along with everything else they learn from us. If we feel our jobs, motherhood, or marriage don't have a real purpose or deeper meaning, then we are teaching *them* to live without purpose and meaning.

A life without purpose is a sad and empty life. Research shows, if our kids don't grow up with some kind of spirituality, faith, or some sort of Higher Power, then they will be lost when chaos strikes. If they see their parents meet each day with little intent or purpose, they will struggle with finding intent and purpose themselves.

I was raised a Catholic, to believe in God, and to pray in hard times. We weren't the family sitting in church every Sunday. Growing up, I was taught to pray and depend on my faith. I was taught by my dad to always ask God to strengthen my back for whatever it is I may have to carry. I'm so glad I did because I know 100% that this is what pulled me through times of heartache when all I saw was doom, gloom, bleakness, and darkness.

My mom took her job as a mother very seriously, too serious in some ways, but I know she saw motherhood as a calling and as a privilege. If she didn't, I don't know how she would have survived some of the times I rebelled when I was a bratty teenager who didn't care about anyone but myself. It doesn't matter what you believe in, but it is important to believe in something other than yourself. You will do yourself and your children such a big favor by living from a spiritual place. How you find that place is up to you; but that is the healthiest thing you can do for your own sanity.

When you live from a spiritual place, the little spats you have with your kids and the things they do that may drive you crazy will help you understand more. You will see the bigger picture and you will know much of your reaction has to do with your inner world and not necessarily what is going on externally. You will become the best version of yourself if you take time for internal reflection in times of madness. Most of what kids go through are usually phases that don't last long. This life is wheels in motion that we don't see or realize most of the time. We are all being shoved forward without recognizing it. What happened today won't be an issue 20 years from now or even a year from now or even next week.

We are here to learn from our kids. In some ways our kids are smarter than we are, if we listen. They are here to teach us to be better people. When we spend time with our kids, we need to slow down and savor that time. When giving them baths and cooking dinner seem more like chores than pleasure, we can look at these daunting tasks in a way that teaches us something. We can find the joy in them or remind ourselves that someday we won't need to do this because our babies will be grown and out of the house. We can then see those tasks as pleasures and feel blessed to have someone for whom to do these things. We are blessed that we have hands to wash dishes and cook; we have clean water to bathe our babies in; and we have enough money and resources to put food on the table.

If we train our minds to look at our daily to-dos and our parenting as a spiritual practice, we will be training our minds to find the joy in these daily tasks. The one thing we won't regret in this life is spending more time with our child or children, following our hearts, and finding joy in our everyday existence. If you see your daily existence as daunting and mundane, that is how you will feel on the inside. If you change your thoughts and look at your daily existence with gratitude, as opportunities, implementing simple spiritual practices and acts of kindness, you will feel not only more peace and contentment, but you also will be living with a new light inside that forgot what it was like to shine. If you watch children play, you can learn from them. They enjoy the present moment no matter what is in front of them, wherever their concentration lies. If we live more like that, we will feel a sense of peace and freedom we didn't know existed.

When you birth your baby, you are reborn yourself into this new role. When we become mothers, everything changes. You are no longer the same woman. Your perception and experience of yourself will be different. Your body will be different. Your hopes, dreams, and desires will be different. It is important to allow yourself time to grieve the loss of the person you were, in order to welcome this new chapter into your life. Your career goals may also change.

Only you can choose what is right for you, so tune out the influence of society and what you think you should be doing, and allow your new self to feel into what is right for you now. I even feel it's true that, as our children enter different phases in their lives, we mourn the loss of the way they used to be. Some of us need to find ourselves once again, especially once our children become teenagers and want their own space and life. Life is constantly changing which means we need to learn how to keep readjusting our sails. Motherhood is a continually unfolding journey that you travel for the rest of your life. We plant different seeds; we just need to know when to water them, tend to them, and most importantly know when to step back, let go, and let nature take its course. We need to quit judging ourselves. Allow yourself time and space to feel and process, without judgment, the experience you are currently having. Many mothers will experience some sort of 'identity crisis' at different stages of motherhood. That is when it is best to journal, pray, reflect, take up yoga, try some new things, or get your creative juices flowing. Asking questions and writing about the complicated emotions that motherhood can stir, can bring you clarity and some grounding into your life path.

When the going gets tough and the road seems long, look deep within the struggle for the spiritual meaning behind it or let go and simply be. Answers will come; peace will follow. Each day upon awakening we make a choice as to how we want to see our day. We can look for the small miracles, the ways in which our kids will push us to better ourselves, or the creativity and beauty all around us that we seem to simply ignore when we are living inside our heads instead of our hearts. Get out of your head and into your life.

Here are some ways in which you can live a deeper spiritual life and look at motherhood as a spiritual journey:

- Pray.
- Meditate.
- Dance literally like no one is watching.
- Read or write poetry.
- Take photographs.
- Paint.
- Sit in stillness.
- Journal, especially if it's a tough day. Set a timer, write in your journal, and see what comes up for you.
- Take a salt bath. Salt is healing and washes away negative energy.
- Set up a mini-shrine somewhere in your house with things that have meaning to you and sit in front of it once or twice a day.
- Write a song or a short story about your current situation.
- Sing as loud as you can.
- Draw.
- Go to a church, chapel, or anywhere that is considered holy space and marvel in the beauty and realm of the spiritual objects placed there. Sit in stillness, bring a journal. Some real insights may come up for you.
- Record your dreams. They are one of the paths to our inner soul.
- Write a letter to someone dear who may have passed away. Our departed loved ones never venture far from us. I believe they are with us and can hear us.
- Cook a delicious meal and place it on beautiful dishes like a work of art.
- Read uplifting material.
- Start a moms' group where you get together once a month to uplift one another.

You get the point. I could go on forever with this list. Most importantly, follow your heart. You've got this! You are doing an excellent job; keep up the good work. The fact that you are reading this shows you want to be the best you can be as a mom. You have likely read books on parenting;

your children love and adore you; you gave them life; you are their rock. Stop being hard on yourself and see the beauty in your everyday existence.

"You are walking a road that has been walked by women from the beginning of time. Open up to that power and access your inner wisdom and strength, and know that you can and you will. Take the time to find balance for yourself, and ask for help. Be brave, be true and you will, with an open heart, guide the next generation to walk this Earth at a higher vibration." - *Claire Michelle*

CHALLENGE: If there is an issue with one or all of your children that keeps coming up and irritating you, write down the problem or irritation. On the same page, list some healthy solutions. Then set a timer for 10-15 minutes and, in that time, journal about where else this irritation may be coming from. It could be something far back in your history.

CHALLENGE: Start with you looking in the mirror every morning/afternoon telling yourself: *Beautiful things are going to happen to me today. Today is a gift. My kids are gifts in my life. My life is unfolding the way it should be. I am loved. My children are loved, and we are safe.* If you say this every day, even if only one of those lines, your life will transform beyond measure.

HEART-OPENING MEDITATION

Sit or lie down comfortably.
Close your eyes.
Exhale in for three and out for five.
Follow the breath.
A beautiful white light is surrounding you.
Your heart is opening to this light.
I am love, I am light, I am gentle with myself and my children, I am strong, I can handle anything that comes my way, I let go and release my troubles to a higher power (God, The Universe, etc.).
Repeat this phrase or one of the phrases or whatever feels comfortable to you for at least three minutes or longer.
Upon awakening, smile and say, *My life flows like the river.*

Chapter 7

STEP 7: I STAND IN MY INNER POWER

I love being a woman. I really do. I have always loved being a woman because I love wearing makeup, dressing up, putting on long flashy earrings, and being courted by a man.

I love those things, of course, but I have a deeper appreciation and love now for being a woman and embracing my femininity. I love supporting other women, collaborating together to help one another become better people, and to achieve our goals and dreams. I love the fact we can tell each other our deepest, darkest secrets and have the ability to console one another, whether that means crying on each other's shoulders, eating a bucket of ice cream together, or smashing the fine wedding china because you are getting a divorce, all while screaming OPA! I never realized how important it is for us women to have each other's backs.

Women who compete constantly with their 'sisters' never really get to enjoy being a woman to the highest level she can. I appreciate all my girlfriends now more than I ever have before, and I appreciate every encounter with other women, whether in business or social situations. We each have gifts and insights to offer and help each other grow.

The more beauty you see in other women, the more beauty you will see in yourself when you look in the mirror. Men are great, and we need them in our lives, but we also need our sisters. It's important to have at least one or two great friends. The more women you encounter, the more you can learn and see in yourself what you never knew existed. The next time you mentally bash another woman, stop and ask yourself: *What about this woman do I appreciate? What about her am I drawn to? What can I learn from her? What about her can I emulate?* We each have something to teach each other.

I've gained a great deal from other women: wisdom, words of advice, and encouragement. This past year, I have opened up to seeing my female relationships differently. My confidence has grown, and I have also made leaps and bounds in my own growth.

Feel sorry for the women you encounter who aren't comfortable around other women. They can only be struggling with their own femininity and haven't fully embraced all parts of themselves. Nor do they feel completely comfortable in their own skin. Rather than disparaging these women, show them your compassion. Treat them as a sister even if it's offering them a smile from across the room, a quick hello, or a quick compliment. Let's build each other up.

There's a beautiful movement afoot in which women are standing up, showing pride for who they are. After years of knocking myself down, thinking I wasn't good enough, I am at last becoming proud of the woman I am, no matter what I do or don't accomplish. God made me in His perfect image and made me unique. I embrace that by honoring who I am.

Here's a quote that puts a smile on my face: "The day I broke up with normal was the first day of my magical life." I intend to blow up that quote and hang it in my house.

Whenever we go through something difficult or compare our lives to others, we assume we must not be normal. Our lives are normal. They may be different from someone else's, but then what is normal? We measure normal based on our expectations. It's OK to have expectations for ourselves but when expectations interfere with our thinking, that is when you need to break up with the expectation. Say to yourself, *Yes, I am normal. I am working towards normal. I simply placed an unrealistic expectation on myself that is getting in the way of my internal happiness.* When you start questioning normalcy in your own life, it indicates you've placed an expectation on yourself.

Let's talk about mornings. I have been paying attention to my morning moods. When the girls wake me up and they are already fighting or in my face saying, "Mommy, Mommy, I want chocolate milk," it's not the best way to wake up. Sometimes I can feel the grouchiness starting to rise in me and I raise my voice. It happened to me this morning. Our morning routine is so important. If you want to start off having a better day, wake up before the kiddos. Give yourself 15 minutes to have your cup of coffee, tea, smoothie, or juice and enjoy the silence. Do a deep breathing exercise or a guided meditation.

Insight Timer is a free meditation app giving you some great meditations. Or read some inspirational quotes to start your day, or a passage in the Bible. Do what gives your heart peace, clears your head, and allows your body to wake up before you start your day. Try this for a week; it will do wonders for your mind, body, and soul. If you have time, take a hot shower and let the water run as you picture it cleansing your body. This will help start your day with ease and clarity.

When you take your morning shower, be present, and focus on how the water feels on your skin. Even though you may be rushed in the morning, be truly present and feel the waterfall cleansing you. Say something positive to yourself as you enter your shower. Also in the morning, set an intention for your day— one word. Today my word was *believe.* I followed it with *believe in the miracles of everyday,* so all through the day I think *believe.* It amazes me how my day will follow suit with the word or intention I set. Most important: give yourself alone time in the morning, even if only a short time to get yourself mentally set and prepared for the day.

If you're married, ask your husband to pitch in with breakfast or lunch making while you get some time alone. Or pick out clothes and have lunches packed the night before so you have more morning time for you. My morning ritual is doing a 10 to 15-minute deep breathing exercise or guided meditation, then I write a few lines in a journal. If there is anything old that needs to be released, I release it, then go to my book where I set my one word for the day. Next, I write down three things for which I'm grateful; then I do a prayer request. Usually I will ask God to help me with something I'm struggling with at the moment. Or I'll ask God for inner strength

If you don't meditate or have a consistent practice, don't worry about doing it right or wrong. There's no one right way; it may be easier to start with a guided meditation. Morning may be our highest level of consciousness.

If you've ever read about or followed highly successful people, you will see a common thread between them: they have a consistent morning ritual. Yours and mine may look different, but it's important to have a good morning routine. Your kids will be grateful for a happier and calmer mom. If you have to, go to bed a little earlier each night. Early morning will be so much more pleasant when you rise and start your day with a positive attitude.

Because I don't have a husband to pass the responsibility torch to when my kids get up before me, and chaos starts, I tell my kids, "I need 10 minutes. I am doing my morning meditation." That may sound selfish to some, but I am teaching my kids healthy morning habits. One, I don't want them to see me on mornings when I don't get to meditate or have my cup of coffee. I can be a real grouch! And, two, I hope someday they will adapt and remember my example. I am subtly teaching them the beauty of self-care and healthy living.

I had such a proud mommy moment a couple weeks ago. As I was picking up my daughter from preschool, I ran into another mother. She said, "You have the most well behaved girls; they are so loving. Whatever you are doing, you are doing right. Can I send my daughter to you to get some tips?"

My face flushed with pride. I replied, "Oh, you're making me cry!" When the girls and I got in the car, I started bawling. I told my daughters how proud I was of them. I really needed to hear her words that day because I had been so critical of my parenting, feeling I was falling short. Her compliment was a game changer for me. I knew I had to quit being so hard on myself. I am learning every day and doing an amazing job.

When I get down on myself and my inner critic emerges to knock me down a peg, I remind myself of that day. I journal about my parenting and what a great mom I am, and how I am leading by example. I may be a single mom, but I have two healthy, happy babies who are not only surviving, but thriving, and that makes me very proud.

When I started this chapter, I said I've had the pleasure of meeting many great women. Since starting to write this book I have met mothers from all races, religions, and walks of life who have shared their beautiful insights with me. Here are some:

This too shall pass.

Let's talk about this. How many times have you thought, *I am going to feel this way forever. This absolutely is hell. This is never going to end.* But did that feeling eventually pass? Of course it did. Life is a series of moments. Life is liquid lucidity, constantly in flow. Almost nothing stays the same; most everything passes. The next time your two year old screams his or her head off, or your 16 year old tells you they hate you, recognize it will pass. Even beautiful moments pass so make sure you are hyper-focused on those moments that you wish you could freeze and last forever.

It's going to be OK.

Just because you are in crisis mode, does not mean you have to spill every little detail to your child or children. Our kids look to us to be their rock, their inner strength. There are some days I think I'm falling apart, suffering from anxiety and feeling sad and depressed; but my kids would never know it. Even if they think their mom seems a little off today, I don't share that information with them. Nor do many women I've met and spoken to.

It is OK for our children to see us sad, or see us a little stressed, but also you want them to feel safe and secure. Make sure you reinforce in your own mind that it will be OK, because it will be OK. Life has a way of working things out, so how you feel right now is not likely to be how you will feel next week or next month. So let's not worry our children. Our kids feed off our personalities and our energy. Speak positively to them. Let them know everything is OK, that we are OK. They don't need to know about mommy and daddy's financial troubles or that Aunt Suzie is dying. I am not suggesting hiding important things from them, but some things should be on a need-to-know basis. When we feed them too much of what goes on in our adult lives, we slowly rob them of their childhood innocence.

Roll with the punches.

This, too, is a difficult one for me. In some areas of my life, I can go with the flow, but motherhood has been challenging while I learn and improve. Change takes time. I used to get anxious when my kids would eat very few fruits and vegetables, or my parents would feed them chocolate before dinner. I have learned to simply let go. Kids will eat when they are hungry. As for my parents, someday I will be a grandparent, and will likely do the same thing. Grandparents don't think like parents, as much as we wish they did. It would certainly make our lives easier, but wishing won't change them. Perhaps we should loosen our grip on things we are adamant about. They could be the very things making our anxiety sky rocket. Not everything is a life or death matter, leaving us in dire straits. Most of our concerns won't matter years from now, days from now, or even hours from now, in some cases.

Turn around and our toddlers soon will be asking for the car keys.

My 17-year-old niece was visiting my parents' house the other day. I looked at her and thought, *Where has the time gone? This is the girl I played with and sang songs with when she was my kids' age. Now she has grown into such a beauty.* I see it happen all around me. We think those difficult stages, times, and ages will last forever. Fortunately, we are wrong that they will last forever. Perhaps we aren't enjoying them because we see the grueling side of parenting, and not the other side. Someday our kids will be all grown up and no longer begging for our attention. We may one day be begging for theirs! Let's hope they won't be too busy for us. As I type this I am reminded of Harry Chapin's song, "Cat's in the Cradle." I believe how we treat our children when they are young will reflect how they behave when they are older.

Hugs and kisses from our children can melt away our stress.

Our kids add stress to our lives, but they can reduce it, too. When I'm stressed or anxious, I probably need my kids more then they need me. I love lying with them and cuddling them. I can actually feel my heartbeat slow down to a steady and joyous pace. The next time you are stressed, distract yourself with some cuddles or a board game with your kids. Involve yourself with activities with your kids and your stress will melt away and you will find a more peaceful, joyous heart. Focusing on our families allows us to regroup and recognize what is most important in this life.

Pick your battles.

Just as we want to be in control of our world, so do our kids. They may be younger, but they are little people with their own minds. Let them make some decisions appropriate to their age. By picking your battles, you let some things go. My six year old does her hair by herself in the morning. It's far from perfect but she wants to do it, and it builds her confidence, so I let her. My four year old wants to wear mismatched clothes to school. Will it hurt anything? No. So I let her do it. Ease up. Choose the battles that count.

Don't get involved in their fights.

I still get involved in my daughters' fights every day, but a wise mom told me I should learn to ignore them so they will figure it out. I am slowly taking this advice.

Children need our love and time.

The quantity of time spent is less important than the *quality* of time we give our children. My kids are at school every day, and on Saturdays they are with their dad. When I am with them, I choose to spend quality time with them. We watch good movies together, do projects, color, play board games, and dance. I try to make it memorable and fun. There are times I am tired and I let them play on their tablets so I can relax, but I make sure this isn't a constant reoccurrence. I want to make memories with my kids, and at four and six, they bond through activity. No matter how old your child is he/she wants and needs your time and your love—it doesn't matter how old they are or how distant they may try to act, they want your love, time, and attention. If you have older kids, ask them what they would like to do for fun and plan a day of fun with them doing an activity you both enjoy. Dinner is great, but getting out and doing a fun activity will work wonders to increase bonding.

Kids talk at night more than any other time.

Have your ears wide open at night, especially right before your child goes to bed. Bedtime is when kids review what happened during their day. Or they may reveal anxiety about the upcoming day, so be there for them when they need to talk. Be sure you tuck them in and ask about their day. I especially ask my six year old if there is anything on her mind she would like to share. Sometimes she has so much to divulge. Had I not asked, she may have kept it to herself. I hear my four year old saying out loud the names of kids in her preschool class. Apparently, that's what was on her mind. When the house is quiet and we're ready for bed, it's normal for us adults to think about what happened that day or what will happen in the days ahead. Our kids are no different. Be available at night for them, talk with them, ask questions, and encourage them to talk.

Kids will never forget the nights we comforted and consoled them when they were at a weak point. This builds a bond between mother and child for a long time to come. My mother was always there for me when I needed to talk, from the time I was a wee thing. Because of the habit she created by always checking in with me about my life, to this day I still tell my mother everything going on in my life. If started at a young age, these habits can last a lifetime. Be as available as possible, especially at bedtime.

Don't stop growing.

Many women I admire gave me the advice to continue learning. Read self-help and inspirational books. Take a class about something that interests you. Never ever stop learning. Our kids teach us every day, so watch closely, and be open to it. When we are lifelong learners, we achieve great things even if it's only for our own personal good. Research shows when we continue to learn, we become better-rounded and happier people. No matter how intelligent you are, there is always more to learn. Think about your next source of inspiration. What would you like to learn next? Forward momentum works wonders for the soul.

Try new things.

So many women have told me that, once their kids were grown and out of the house, they had no clue who they were besides being moms. They shared with me it was a very scary time; so I asked mothers who had a good sense of who they were once their children left the house, and they said they carved out time for trying new activities and never quit trying new things. This helped them discover a deeper sense of self, and although these mothers were sad when their kids left, they were not lost. They had activities they enjoyed; they made lots of new friends along the way, and had a better sense of self. Never stop discovering new things, new foods, and new activities. Our kids want to see us grow and flourish right alongside them. Make a list of some fun, cool things you could try. If you're interested in yoga, zumba, or photography, check them out.

Be sexy at any age.

I had the pleasure of meeting a wonderful 80-year-old woman named Joan who feels women can be sexy at any age. Even at her age, she still has men pursuing her. Embrace each decade with confidence and grace. The reason people think they aren't as attractive as they age is only because they trained their minds to think that way. We can be sexy at any age. If we believe it, we can achieve it. I believe beauty starts on the inside. Have you ever seen a person who looks beautiful on the outside, but they have an ugly demeanor and attitude? It doesn't take long to see the ugliness when you encounter these people. The opposite is true. Someone who isn't a GQ or beauty queen on the outside can still be incredibly attractive when they have inner beauty. Embrace the looks God gave you. Take care of yourself. Exercise, avoid smoking, and drink plenty of water. Do all those things, but don't stress over a wrinkle. Embrace your face! List all the good things each decade brings you. You could do this every year on your birthday. If you ever feel low about your looks, or your age, write down the features you love about yourself both on the inside and out.

Don't be afraid of dark thoughts.

I've never met anyone who didn't have dark thoughts from time to time. Live from your light and don't let darkness consume you. When dark thoughts come up, acknowledge them for what they are and let them go. Psychologists and spiritual gurus say we are not our thoughts. As I become more insightful with age, I see and understand this more. Our thoughts could come from anyone: our mom, dad, brother, sister, friend, neighbor, or a lady in line at the supermarket. Be savvy when the dark thoughts come. Don't let them scare you. Instead, mentally label them junk or trash, and picture yourself crumpling them up as paper and throwing them into a trash can labeled Junk. Or picture writing the thought on paper and burning the paper. Label thoughts that are dark and do not fit you, and see yourself getting rid of them. If they keep coming back, don't let your thoughts scare you. They are harmless, can't hurt you, and will not last forever. If you have a hard time reeling your thoughts in, or they are causing you anguish, please seek professional help such as medical or therapeutic counseling. It takes a strong and brave person to reach out for help.

A beautiful woman once told me: *"A coward dies a thousand times before his death, but the valiant face death but once."* I've held onto this beautiful sentiment since she shared it with me.

One day I went to her and discussed with her how I was nervous about losing my mother. Although my mom is in good health, she is getting older and I secretly worry about her sometimes, to the point where it keeps me up at night. No matter our age, we still want and need our mothers. I hope my daughters will feel the love for me that I feel for my mom. This woman looked at me and said, "Jennie, my mom used to share this saying with me. Once I heard it, it has stuck with me."

It is so true. We can make up scary scenarios in our head and waste away beautiful days filled with worry, or we can enjoy our days and enjoy those we love and not face things until they actually come up. So many things I have worried about that never came to fruition; so why torture ourselves? But that is exactly what we do.

When something happens that needs our attention, we somehow have an inner strength that carries us through; but when we worry about something that has yet to happen, we have nothing to fight with. It's a made-up worry. We just keep ruminating and exhausting ourselves for no real reason. That's not self-love, so the next time you have something negative in your mind that hasn't happened, think of this saying. Breathe and show yourself enough love to move on and let it go. Worry is a learned behavior. It takes time to develop a habit of worrying, but it can be undone. Try not to model the excessive worry trait to your kids. Believe this quote, live by it, and hopefully you will find yourself worrying far less.

HALT: Hungry, Angry, Lonely, and Tired.

The next time you find yourself in an internal struggle, stop and ask yourself: Are you hungry, angry, lonely, or tired? Your answer will make it easier for you to give yourself the proper self-care you may need. This is used in substance abuse support groups, but it is useful for anyone. Another life coach shared this with me and said she uses this in her own life. She wasn't an addict, but she said it still helped her take better care of herself.

Having awareness is a beautiful thing. When we are aware of what is going on with us, we can help ourselves to feel empowered to fulfill our own needs or ask for help. If you're feeling really tired, ask your husband if he can leave work a little early or clean up after dinner while you take a bath. Remember, sister, self-care and self-awareness start with you. If you don't treat yourself with love, care, and respect, then who will? HALT helps you determine the best way to take care of yourself.

Many of us will make up excuses like, "I don't have anyone to babysit, or little Suzie will only let me put her to sleep or she will be a wreck." Don't make excuses. You are worth it. Don't let yourself down. The more love and care you give yourself, the more your children will benefit. You are filling your cup so you have more love to pour into their lives.

Say YES to help.

Always say yes to help. When Bobby's mom says she will take your son to the game, say YES. When Mrs. Miller asks if you need anything from the grocery store, and you really need milk, say YES. When Linda offers to babysit while you take a nap, say YES, please. You get my point. Say yes anytime it will make your life a little easier. What's the other benefit of this? The people helping us also get a sense of satisfaction for being able to help.

I used to have a hard time asking for help, but now I do it easily; and I also offer help when I see other mothers in need. It's great to receive when you need it, but you also want to be a giver, too. Having a relationship with other mothers where you each give and take, helping each other in need forms a strong bond. We women need connection and a sense of community. Did you know that the more people do for you, the more they like you?

Sometimes I think people tend to talk only about how hard motherhood can be and not about the beautiful aspects of motherhood. Motherhood is the most beautiful thing I have ever experienced. Yes, it can be hard at times for all mothers. That's why it's important to find calm and connect with ourselves as humans first every day.

A mother is the most beautiful creature in the world, and while some negative thoughts and feelings will come up, that means little. They are like clouds passing through. It is best to try and see our children in the most positive light.

Write down the beautiful and unique things you love about them at every stage in their life, the qualities that make them unique. I have been 100 percent blessed by being a mom. I think God trusts me to take care of these innocent, beautiful beings. I embrace knowing they are healing me and helping me as much as I help them. Our kids' lives help us heal and learn wonderful things about ourselves. Mommies and daddies are blessed. Cherish every stage, because you know these stages do not last.

"The best place to cry is in a mother's arms."—Jodi Picoult

Let your instincts be your guide. Our instincts are our inner wisdom. At the end of the day, only we know what is best for us and our families. God created instincts to be our moral compass and to help us know when we are on the right path for our lives.

CHALLENGE: When you take your morning shower, be present, and focus on how the water feels on your skin. Even though you may be rushed in the morning, be truly present and feel the waterfall cleansing you. Say something positive to yourself as you enter your shower. Also in the morning, set an intention for your day; one word. Today my word was *believe.* I followed it with *believe in the miracles of everyday,* so all through the day I think *believe.* It amazes me how my day will follow suit with the word or intention I set. Most important: give yourself alone time in the morning, even if only a short time to get yourself mentally set and prepared for the day.

CHALLENGE: We talked about how important it is to never stop learning. Find something new to learn about.

CHALLENGE: Within the next 30 days, try something new, whether it is a new food, activity, exercise program, new route to work, etc. Try to do this at least once a month. You will be amazed at how refreshing this can be.

INNER POWER MEDITATION:

Find a comfortable spot.

Close your eyes.

Follow the breath in and out.

Imagine being engulfed by a light filled with many colors.

This light is your Guide.

This light is filling every inch of your body with Wisdom and Inner Strength.

Repeat these phrases, breathing in and out between each one:

I stand in my inner power, I am worthy and wise.

I will live up to my full potential.

I trust in a higher power to give me the strength I need.

I shine bright.

Take a few more deep breaths.

Slowly open your eyes.

This meditation tends to be more powerful when followed with a short prayer of gratitude.

Chapter 8

SINGLE MOM LIFE

This chapter I hold very dear and close to my heart. I was not always a single mom, but when my daughter, Abriana, was one month old, my husband and I decided to call it quits. That was one of the most painful and terrifying times of my life. There I was with two babies, a one month old and a two year old, a failed marriage, and the realization that I must now do this all on my own.

Fortunately, I had help from my parents—a lot of help—but it's not the same as having a partner in the same home with you that you can count on for support in the middle of the night when you have two crying or sick babies. Now it was only me, and it was downright terrifying.

I remember some nights lying in bed with tears rolling down my face and I would just pray that God would give me the inner strength to get through this dark time in my life. I call it a dark time because of all the pain and loneliness I was feeling. I have to be honest—when my marriage finally ended, and papers were signed, I did feel a sense of relief at its conclusion. I started to feel hopeful for the first time in a long time. I knew being on my own with two small children was going to be a struggle, but I also knew the pain I felt towards the end of my marriage was finally turning into hope for a brighter future.

I wouldn't wish divorce on my worst enemy. Anyone who has been through a divorce has experienced intense emotion surrounding the beginning, middle, and end of a crumbling marriage. Divorce can make you feel that you are waking up in the middle of a nightmare. Then I think, what is worse, staying in a marriage that no longer serves you, or being on your own and actually creating the life you want and always dreamed of for yourself? I will choose the latter even though it can be harder. You are now at the helm of your household, without backup. It's all you, whether you are disciplining the kids to sit down to dinner, helping them do their homework, or giving midnight feedings while your other child cries because she needs you, too.

It took a while to get where I am at today but with prayers, journaling, and help, here I am. It does get easier and now I live every day with excitement because I know I'm where I'm meant to be, creating a life I've always dreamed of. Did I dream on my wedding day that I would be raising my kids alone? Uh, no.

I knew I wanted my kids to see a mom who was happy, content, and living her best life. Did I ever regret getting divorced? Yes, which is very normal. I searched for a way we could make it work, and I wonder if I could have done more. I would cycle through thinking, *It could never have worked,* to *Maybe it could have,* to carrying shame and embarrassment, feeling like a failure. *My marriage now ended, I am a single mom, and I don't want to be a single mom.*

When I would search my soul, and peel back the onion of my emotions, I realized my marriage ending was the best thing that ever happened to me and my ex-husband. I no longer think I could have saved my marriage; I now think we were meant to have our kids and then go our separate ways. I wouldn't have been happy living the way we had been living. I believe in forever and persevering, but not if it means holding yourself back from happiness. Years ago women stayed in unhappy, unfulfilling marriages because they believed they had to. These women suppressed other parts of themselves. They let their passions die and pushed away their own happiness for the sake of saving their family. All the while, their children watched them, thinking their mothers' choices were OK, and then either copying the behavior, or being turned off to marriage because of what they saw their parents go through.

Neither of those scenarios are good, so when we teach our kids that it is important to preserve and ride the marriage wave of challenges, it's also important to teach them to stay true to who they are. Value your happiness and the more content, peaceful, and happy you are, the better life you are giving your children, even if that means doing it alone. If you are married and happen to be torn about staying in your marriage, try first to make it work. Go to counseling, go on dates, have more sex, or if sex is nonexistent, rekindle the flame, and try to communicate more effectively. Only if you see none of those things working, or if you have tried everything and don't have a willing partner, or if there is no longer any love left, then DO NOT BE AFRAID to leave. You'll be OK. I promise you.

Being a single mom isn't easy but I don't at all see that my life has been shortchanged. I have come to accept my life as it is. As soon as I did that and stopped thinking married women around me must have it better or easier, I understood that isn't always the case. We are all walking our own path; it's about accepting where we are on that path at the moment.

That is exactly what I did: *I accepted*. I *own* being a single mom. Authenticity is about owning who you are. If you believe as I do that everything happens for a reason, then we are where we are meant to be. Challenges are lessons we need to learn for our own personal growth. If you see life as a school, and we are the students, then you will find acceptance more easily. If you don't believe things happen for a reason, you may have a harder time reaching acceptance. At some point, you will. And when you do it is liberating.

When we learn to accept what is, we free ourselves from anxiety, pain, and overwhelm. You have the power to change the things you can change. Don't wait if there is something in your life that isn't working for you. Change it; do not wait.

The one thing we can't change is being a mom. God trusted us enough to raise our sweet babies and put them in our care. However, if for some reason you can't care for your child, please tell someone you know and trust to care for your children. I hope you can, and because you are reading this book it shows how invested you are and dedicated to being the best mom you can be. If you see your life isn't going well and you don't feel you are the best you can be for your children, start now by listing what isn't working. What do you want to change? Then list the specific changes you desire, then break them down into manageable baby steps, and get moving.

I can only hope you aren't in an abusive relationship and that you know your worth. I have worked with many single moms who have trusted me and have told me personal details of their situations. What pains me is the number of single moms who will stay in abusive relationships with either the father of their children or with a boyfriend, just so they don't feel alone. This makes me want to cry. Being on your own helps you determine who you are as a woman, a mom, and a human being.

When you have the pleasure of being on your own for a while, you learn more about yourself. You learn to appreciate *you,* and you begin to enjoy your own company, which is very important if someday you want to enter a *healthy* relationship.

If you do not love yourself or enjoy your own company, or can't be alone, you may continue to repeat the same unhealthy behavior. Until we admit to ourselves where we are lacking, we will continue to make the same relationship mistakes.

I had to finally admit to myself that in the past I chose men who were incapable of really being emotional available, and who came from childhood trauma. I chose them because I have a big heart and wanted to help them fix their severely wounded hearts. Instead, I got my heart broken each time. Regardless of whether I called it quits or they did, it was still painful and I ended up with a broken heart. I know now I will choose a healthier man. I want an equal partner with whom I share much in common.

It took me years to see and understand the mistakes I made in past relationships. Once the truth smacked me in the face, I asked myself: *How do I change this toxic relationship pattern I created?* That's when I started doing a lot of inner work. I read a pile of books, I wrote all my painful feelings in my journal, I got on my knees and prayed to break this unhealthy cycle I have continued, and most important of all, I took a hard look at the way I felt about myself.

I'm all for dating as a single mom; it can be fun and uplifting. When dating, be sure you are in a solid, grounded place and not dating out of desperation to find someone. I don't want that for you. You deserve better and your children deserve better.

Dating as a single mom is liberating, but sometimes feels like you are living a double life because it's better that your kids not know when you go out on dates. When a relationship becomes serious, that will be the time to have them meet. Dating helps you feel good about yourself, sexy, and feminine.

It is important to get out of the house, meet new people, and try new and exciting things. Do not close your heart; your children want you to be happy. Know that a man doesn't have the power to make you happy. He should merely be adding to the happiness you already feel. When you date as a single mom it gives you an extra dose of empowerment, like, *Wow, I can have it all.* And you can!

Any man who can't accept your children will not be the right man for you. If a man says he isn't interested in meeting the kids, or will never get married, or doesn't want to do family things, believe him. You won't change him. When you're ready to date again, prepare by listing what qualities are important to you. List the qualities you want in a partner, what you need, and also what behaviors you don't want. Don't waver on the things on your list. The best man will meet 80 percent of your list. Nobody is perfect, but you want your man to be perfect for you.

I was unsure about adding this experience of my life to this chapter, but I choose to be honest and raw, so here it goes.

About a year after my divorce I met a man who was very attractive, successful, and charming. When we met I was new to the dating scene and initially was looking only to have fun, but because I am relationship-oriented, a part of me hoped this man would be the right one for me, my life partner. He lived about an hour away, so he would come see me once a week when my kids were with their dad. Then it became twice a week and I would also make the trip to see him, too. It was exciting. I felt passionate about him and the way things were progressing.

And yet the whole time we were together, I had an instinct something was not right. I hung in, although I would lie next to him, feel his pain, feel his distance, and feel his guard up. I talked myself out of these nagging feelings. I believed by giving this guy enough love and attention, I could break through those walls. I was so naive. He did ask me to marry him, which I hadn't expected because of his uncertain behavior. When I said yes it felt forced, it didn't feel natural or real. I ignored my inner feelings.

What I was picking up on was we were not a good fit for each other. I still don't know why he proposed to me when I knew deep down he was not ready for a commitment with a divorced woman with two children. This man was never married and had no children. His longest relationship was only eight months. The signs were there that a commitment to a woman wasn't his strong suit.

I knew it very early on. I knew who was standing in front of me, who was whispering sweet nothings in my ear, but I chose to ignore it. Needless to say, that relationship came to an end. At first, when it ended, I was crushed. I still held on to hope, but as I started doing my inner work, I realized I wasn't ready for a serious commitment either. I had not been in a good place. I still had pain to sort out from my marriage ending. I was focusing on finding someone else because I wanted a traditional family again. I wanted someone to come home to, and someone to come home to us. What I hadn't done back then was the inner work that I needed to do.

When I met my now ex-fiancé I was vulnerable. I was broken. I wanted to fill the spaces in my heart with something other than the pain I felt from a crumbling marriage. My priorities were not in the right place.

I have since met women who, as soon as their marriage ended, wanted to find someone rather quickly. I had been like them. That is Mistake #1. When a relationship ends and right away we want to find someone else, that's when we need to pause and find ourselves instead. That's when we need to be grateful and learn from our broken marriage and get to a healthy place again. Being a single mom can be challenging, so we think it will be easier to have someone in our lives. It will *if* it is the right person, but not if it is the *wrong* person.

I am now in such a good place. I feel happy, content, and at peace. I can finally say I love myself and accept myself exactly as I am. I live 100 percent authentically. Of course, I would like to meet someone at some point. I am a relationship-type girl, but if it does not happen for a long time, I am completely OK with that. This is where I want you to arrive before you get back out there again.

When you are in a place of self-love, acceptance, and contentment, that is when—if it is meant to be—you will meet a healthy man who will add to your life, and not drain you, exploit you, or constantly take from you.

As for the fiancé I spoke about to whom I was with for two years of my life, I don't regret the experience for a second. He was one of my greatest teachers. Time is never wasted if we learn from our past mistakes and relationships and grow from the experience.

The most important lesson I learned from that relationship was to trust myself, trust my instincts, and walk away when it doesn't feel right. I pass that wisdom along to you. No matter if a man seems perfect for you, if you feel instinctively that something is not right, or you believe he isn't The

One, do not fight it; embrace that feeling. Be true to yourself and move on. Be patient, love yourself, and the right person will come along. First you need to put yourself in a place where you are OK no matter what. I wish you a lot of love and luck dating. Be open to receive. You will find a meditation on love and openness at the end of this chapter.

Don't let anyone tell you not to pursue your dreams just because you are a single mom. We all have dreams. From some dreams we can make a career. Being a single mom doesn't mean you have to give up your dream of owning your own business, writing a book, going back to school, or whatever else your heart desires. Whatever your dream may be, go for it! It may take you a little longer to get there, but you can do it, girl. Do you know how proud your children will be when they see their mom is accomplishing her dreams? As you do, you will be teaching them how to persevere and follow their own dreams. Start today, even if you start small.

My dream was to coach the single mom to live her BEST LIFE NOW and to travel around the country for speaking engagements that empower single mothers. To start small, I started a local support group for single moms, meeting on the third Saturday of the month. I invite speakers to come and chat. Most of them are, or were, single moms and they inspire these newly single or seasoned mothers who are struggling.

I began writing this book when Viviana was a baby. I started it because of my own struggle, and for my sanity and healing, as time went on. I kept writing because I was no longer shamed by my story. I wanted to enjoy sharing it with other mothers. My point is don't give up on your dreams or your passions; keep them alive by starting small and working toward a bigger vision. I don't have much free time but I carve out time one to two days a week to build my dream career, step by step.

My daughters stay with their dad only one day a week, on Saturday. Usually I spend that day playing catch up from the week and sometimes I am just exhausted and want to lie on my couch and binge watch TV, but if I have a date with my dreams, I make an effort to stick with it. Don't let yourself get stuck in a dead end job. We all have bills to pay, but by opening yourself up to living a passionate life, you live up to your full potential. Put some of the money you have or earn off to the side to save for your own business, if that is your aspiration, or for buying more art supplies to sell your art or crafts on Etsy. Whatever it may be, plan for it, dream it, and you will achieve it.

It is good for every human on the planet to have some sort of spiritual life. We can get through challenges more easily when we believe in something bigger than ourselves, but this is crucial for the life of a single mom. So many times I have kneeled down and begged God for inner strength. I would write, pray, and meditate. I started doing loving-kindness meditations, and I searched for forgiveness in my heart. It is very unhealthy to hold on to anger and resentment, especially toward the father of your children. You do yourself a disservice by holding on to anger and resentment.

You actually hurt your child as well as yourself. Your kids know instinctively when you have a personal quarrel with the other parent, and that is detrimental to them. Spirituality comes into play when we believe in something bigger than ourselves and can look at our lives to try to make sense out of why this is happening to us.

Here's where acceptance comes back in: accepting where you are on your life's journey and letting go of control of everything. You can never control another human being, especially your ex. I now have respect for my ex. I can see the forest for the trees. He gave me two beautiful daughters, and even though I don't always agree with how he does things, I have learned to accept him and his parenting style. My kids love him. He is their dad, and that's what matters.

My number one priority is that my children are happy. My ex-husband gave me the best gift I can ever ask for from God. He gave me the gift of being a mother, and I cannot thank him enough for that. We created two beautiful, healthy children together. I know it was time for us to move on from one another and co-parent our children, living separate lives.

When we don't see the beauty in ugliness and pain, we suffer tremendously. Even when we do see the beauty, it is still hard for us, but we can acknowledge that things will get better. This was a life lesson I needed to learn. Holding on to bitterness, anger, and resentment will bring you down; and the only one who is hurt by harboring those nasty feelings is you.

When we live a life of anger and are holding a tight grip on the past, we aren't living up to our full potential. We are just creatures on a hamster wheel, comfortable spinning around in our own misery. I don't want this to become you, me, or anyone else.

If you believe in a Higher Power, take time to record the lessons you learned that helped you. If you still hold a lot of anger or resentment toward your baby daddy, try to accept his limitations. It is hard, but you can do it. If you don't believe in a Higher Power, you can still write down what you learned from the ending of each relationship you've had and how being a mom has helped you grow.

Without a good vision of moving forward, it is easy for a single mom to get stuck in the bitterness and sourness that life can bring. It is easy for a single mom to feel hopeless when all she focuses on is putting food on the table. There is always something to be hopeful for. Even if your hope is merely to be able to get out of bed in the morning, you can start small with a little bit of hope but make sure you have some hope.

Please do not be afraid to ask for help. It takes a village. When you are struggling, reach out to someone and do not be ashamed. Don't be shy about letting your kid's dad know, *Hey I need extra help—I am struggling right now.* Own that request. After all, who better to pitch in extra help with your child than their dad? Asking for help is being smart. We all need help and asking isn't a sign of weakness—it is a sign of strength. You need that two-hour power nap in the afternoon because it is going to be just you at four in the morning when little Jack is crying and needs his mommy. Start asking for help now, and when a safe, close person asks to take the kids for the day or a couple hours say YES. You can always get something done in that time. Even if that something is nothing, it's still something—you are recharging your energy. Trust me, you will be happy you said yes and you will be better ready for them when they get home after you had your much-needed break. Say YES to life. When you start saying yes more to accepting help, you will notice your life will flow with more ease and grace. By putting ease at the forefront of your life, you will slowly start to live a better one. This life needs to not only be enjoyable for your family but for you as well.

When I became a single mom, I was scared. But I was also empowered. I felt free and strong and as though like the world was my oyster. The days of having to answer to someone else were GONE. I have to tell you that part felt amazingly great.

You are a single mom; you are not a victim. You are a strong, capable woman who I have faith in. The fact you are reading this book tells me you are on the way to wanting to better your life. Being a successful single mom takes a strong woman, a brave woman. It doesn't matter how you ended up in the single mom life—by choice or through divorce. Our lives may all look a little different, but I can guarantee you we have a lot of the same challenges, thoughts, and feelings of being overwhelmed. I also know we all share hopes and dreams. Mine may be different from yours but I know you have them.

I hope you dig deep and explore what you want from this life. What kind of legacy do you want to leave behind for your children? Remember there is no rush. One foot in front of the other. That is all it takes. I want to empower you like I empower the women who come to my single mom support group. You are special and I know there is a beautiful life waiting for you on the horizon. Start small, sun up to sun down, my dear friend.

If you are interested in starting a single mom empowerment group in your area, please contact me so I can help get you started. Also, if you are interested in 1:1 Coaching, please visit my website www. singlemomempowered.com. Also look for me on Instagram under Jennie Askins or Single Mom Life Empowerment.

Here are some of my Empowering Affirmations:

I have all the inner strength I need to get through my day.
I am a great mom to my children.
I am patient and show my kids a lot of love.
My kids are watching me by example and I am a great example for them.
I am where I am meant to be.
Life is constantly changing and great things are coming my way.
I live in the moment, from sun up to sun down.
I am very lucky there are many beautiful pieces to being a single mom.
I accept my life as it is.

CHALLENGE: On a sheet of paper write down: *I accept where I am at this moment. I accept the good times and bad.* You will be amazed how much grace you will gain by doing this exercise frequently and how your life will change for the better. Little miracles will start to happen.

CHALLENGE: "Faith as small as a mustard seed" is all you need. If you like to journal, you can write daily about how your hope and faith are growing. Write about the little miracles that happen in your day. Miracles can be as small as, *I finally could sit down and enjoy a cup of coffee...* or *The smell of my morning coffee made me smile...* or *My son touched my heart this morning when he told me I was his favorite person.* You see where I am going with this: it starts small, and before you know it, your life will be on fire with these everyday miracles. I know being a single mom can be very rough some days. It is important to live sun up to sun down on those days.

MEDITATION TO OPEN THE HEART:

We will be using the mantra OM, which helps to open up the Heart Chakra.

Put one hand on your heart and one hand on your stomach.

Breathe gently, following the breath in and out

As the breath flows in and out, imagine that it is flowing deep within the heart center.

Start chanting OM quietly or aloud, and let the vibration of OM fill your body.

OM is about feeling rather than thinking.

Once you've reached an inner peace, a feeling of oneness...

Say quietly or aloud:

My heart is open; I am open to receive.

I am Creating Space in my Heart.

Anytime you feel distracted, go back to chanting OM.

When you are ready, come out of the meditation gently and slowly.

Give yourself a couple minutes to regroup.

LOVING-KINDNESS MEDITATION:

Find a quiet place with no distractions.

Sit in a comfortable position.

Breathe gently and recite these phrases for your own well-being:

May I be filled with love.

May I be safe.

May I live with ease.

As you say these phrases, picture a white light surrounding you with warmth and love.

Now picture a person you love or care about and recite the same phrases:

May you be filled with love.

May you be safe.

May you live with ease.

Now picture a person you do not like:

May you be filled with love.

May you be safe.

May you live with ease.

To be able to love another always starts first with loving yourself. If we can't love ourselves, we can't entirely love another. Many blessings.

In Closing

Thank you for taking the time to read my book. The future is now in your hands. Of course you want your child to look back with fondness at their childhood. And you'll want to look back at your own life someday and know that you took time to slow down, spent time caring for yourself, and found great joy in watching your kids grow up. If you examine your life now and realize you're heading in a direction that you don't like, why not start on a new, positive path today? You are creating a legacy. For yourself. And for your family.

I am so grateful I had the opportunity to write this book and help you on your journey. I've loved sharing what I've learned, both professionally and personally. As you strive to be the best version of yourself that you can be, I hope you can feel the love I am sending to you.

This is our journey. We are constantly learning. We're brave women who can be open to growth opportunities and change. I wrote this book with honesty and love—I wrote it to share and connect with women like myself who are looking for the meaning in their lives. I look forward to sharing more with you in the future. No matter what life brings, I have faith you will always find your way.

Much Love and Gratitude,
Jennie

I would love to stay in touch! Please visit my website at SingleMomEmpowered.com or email me at singlemomlifeeriepa@gmail.com

THE MOST POWERFUL CONNECTION YOU WILL EVER MAKE IS WITHIN YOURSELF.

Being a mother is far from easy. But motherhood can become effortless when you are living every day from a place of inner strength, peace, and confidence. As mothers, we must stop trying to look outside ourselves for happiness and fulfillment and realize that we can achieve peace, balance, and true joy by connecting within—and getting to know ourselves.

In Connecting Within, Creative Coach Jennie Askins will help moms find positive ways to look at parenting. With a meditation and a personal growth challenge at the end of each chapter, Askins will help guide you and give you the clarity you need to become the best mom you can be.

This book will help you:
• Become calmer and more confident.
• Bring about positive change in the way you parent.
• Help you create a better balance in your life.
• Adopt more positive ways of thinking.
• Start looking at motherhood as a true spiritual calling.
• Accept where you are on the journey.

When we first become mothers, we sometimes fall into the trap of thinking we no longer matter. Askins reassures you that you do matter and that you deserve to be happy. Motherhood is a long and winding path but it is possible to enjoy every minute of it. This book will share techniques for self-care that will enable you to enjoy a more peaceful motherhood journey.

Visit the author at SingleMomEmpowered.com.

Printed in the United States
By Bookmasters